The Psychology of Happiness and Well - Being

Super Proven Techniques that Work and Some that Don't

The Psychology of Happiness and Well – Being
Super Proven Techniques that Work and Some that Don't

By Vali Nasser

Copyright © 2010

Online editions may also be available for this title. For more information email: valinasser@gmail.com

All rights reserved by the author. No part of this publication can be reproduced, stored in a retrieval system, or transmitted in any form or by any means, electronic, mechanical, photocopying, recording or otherwise, without the prior permission of the publisher and/ or author.

ISBN: 978-0-557-25989-2

Acknowledgements

I am grateful to my parents (both gone) for my existence. I am grateful to my grandfather, ages ago, for teaching me to question things. I am grateful to my wife and children for their feedback and encouragement and finally, I am grateful to my friends for constantly challenging me.

Introduction...7

Chapter 1..10

Standard Approaches That Don't Work....................10

Chapter 2..15

Neuro - Linguistic Programming (NLP) - New Psychology or Mumbo Jumbo?..15

Chapter 3..19

The Placebo Effect – Use Alternative Therapy as a Last Resort...19

Chapter 4..23

The Mathematics of a Successful Marriage...........23

Chapter 5..28

Smiling and Laughter...28

Chapter 6..32

Increasing your Happiness - Initial Thoughts......32

Chapter 7..42

Optimism..42

Chapter 8..46

Prayer and Compassion..46

Chapter 9..52

Mindfulness Meditation..52

Chapter 10..60

Punching Pillows Does not Quell Your Anger......60

Chapter 11 65
Giving and Volunteering 65

Chapter 12 70
Go with the Flow 70

Chapter 13 75
Forgiving 75

Chapter 14 78
Exercise 78

Chapter 15 83
Anxiety, Social Anxiety & Depression – CBT May Help You 83

Chapter 16 89
Reduce Your Risk of Heart Disease and Strokes by Increasing your Social Connectedness and Controlling your Anger 89

Chapter 17 96
Understanding the Psychology of Money and Managing Debt 96

Chapter 18 102
After Thoughts and Concluding Remarks 102

About the Author

Vali Nasser has a degree in Cognitive and Social Psychology as well as a degree in Mathematics and Physics. In addition, through his consulting experience in Organization Development he has gained an advanced qualification in Change Management. In the last five years he has been practicing Mindfulness Meditation and is presently semi-retired.

In this new book he has researched various psychological methods that claim to remove our mental distress, as well as those that claim to give us more happiness. In particular he has evaluated studies in Psycho-Analysis, Cognitive Behavior Therapy, Mindfulness Training as well as the burgeoning field of Positive Psychology.

He is skeptical of methods, however appealing they may be, that have not been scientifically validated.

The author hopes that his new book 'The Psychology of Happiness and Well-Being' will be of interest to readers who want to know those techniques that actually work as well as those that, don't or may be suspect.

His first book 'Speed Mathematics Using the Vedic System' has had a significant following and has been translated into Japanese as well as Chinese. The author has also worked as a teacher of mathematics.

Introduction

The Psychology of Happiness and Well-being is not a quick fix guide to happiness. Its main emphasis is to point out the findings on happiness studies that have withstood the rigor of 'controlled' studies.

We will see that this approach is important, as sometimes intuitively appealing techniques that initially show promise, fail to show the benefits claimed, when put to scientific scrutiny.

For example, we will see that some anger management techniques such as 'punching pillows' that claim to give a cathartic release actually increase anger even more.

We will also see that affirming the positive like 'day by day I will get better and better' might actually make you feel worse.

We will see that simply visualizing outcomes rarely leads to achieving our desired goals. Further we will investigate whether 'mirroring' techniques that claim to build deep rapport are any better than good old fashioned 'listening' skills.

If that is not enough, you will also find you cannot always just stop worrying. You probably already know that the dictum 'Stop worrying and you will be fine' doesn't actually work.

Unfortunately, the self-help industry has been guilty of pushing many quick fix solutions that rarely work, although judging from the popularity of self-help books it seems we want to believe that their approaches do in fact work.

We will also revisit traditional 'psychoanalysis' whose approaches and constructs have repeatedly been demonstrated to be invalid. We will question some of the techniques used by Neuro-Linguistic Programming and see how the Placebo effect can really fool us into believing that a treatment such as homeopathy works.

On a more optimistic note we will investigate a number of tried and tested techniques, in Cognitive Behavior Therapy and in the field of Positive Psychology that can actually help us improve our well-being as well as make us happier.

Some of the approaches from Positive Psychology may seem like common sense yet others may sound like dictates of 'moral' philosophy or practices from the virtues tradition. But the interesting finding is that practiced in an appropriate way theses approaches and methods do confer tangible happiness and health benefits.

The burgeoning field of Positive Psychology has re-affirmed some important truths and put them on a scientific footing. We will visit 'gratitude' studies by researchers, such as Martin Seligman and Sonja Lyubomirsky, et al. We will look at the notion of positivity ratio by Barbara Fredrickson and her research into the 'broaden and build' hypothesis for increasing happiness and resilience. We will look at the success formula for a happy marriage by John Gottman, the facial feedback hypothesis in 'smiling' activities by Bernstein et al, and also look at some approaches to anger management that actually work.

Although we will see that it is important to undertake activities that give us fun, make us smile more, and sometimes be silly, for a deeper level of happiness and contentment, you will find that you also need to involve yourself in tasks and activities that increase your 'flow' as well as those that give you 'meaning' and provide 'social engagement'.

Although the book has several approaches that can add to your happiness, for best results you will need to pick a few techniques that you feel comfortable with and that you believe will work for you.

I hope that the readers of the book will increase their happiness and well - being.

Standard Approaches That Don't Work

In all affairs it's a healthy thing now and then to hang a question mark on the things you have long taken for granted

Bertrand Russell

Chapter 1

Standard Approaches That Don't Work

When things go wrong and we find ourselves incessantly worrying over the same thing we may find ourselves saying 'I must pull myself together' or 'be more positive'. Our well-meaning friends and family members will, of course, reinforce this by saying 'stop worrying and you'll be all right'.

Society expects us to pull ourselves together. Some self- help books don't help either. "Think positively, remove those troublesome thoughts and you'll be fine", they proclaim. The reality is that the harder we try the more difficult it is to suppress unwanted thoughts. It turns out that the very thoughts that you are trying to 'stop' keep coming back with a vengeance.

This failure to suppress unwanted thoughts makes us feel even worse. If we happen to be a depressive type we may even feel that we are a loser or that we are not strong- minded, as we can't seem to control our thoughts.

What is the evidence that thoughts are not easy to suppress?

In the mid 1980's Daniel Wegner carried out a thought suppression exercise. He had come across a quote by Dostoyevsky in Winter Notes on Summer Impressions: 'Try to pose for yourself this task: not to think of a polar bear, and you will see that the cursed thing will come to mind every minute'

To test this hypothesis, Dan Wegner asked a group of participants to try hard not to think of a white bear, as well as food or a stereo - type. Participants found this task hard to do. Typically, they found that if they tried to suppress a thought, the same or similar thoughts came flooding back which in turn became even harder to banish. This seemed to suggest that Dostoyevsky was right.

Dan Wegner also asserts that when one is anxious or in a low mood it is almost impossible to think positively as one is so pre-occupied with one's current thoughts. The popular belief of thinking positive thoughts in order to improve one's low mood does not usually work.

Thoughts, as Buddha discovered are automatic and controlling them by merely suppressing them is almost impossible.

Wegner's research in turn confirms that thought processes are automatic. We have countless thoughts every day and we tend to get stuck with ones that shock us, or those thoughts that we try to suppress.

Traditional psychoanalysis, another approach for resolving human psychological problems and increasing our well - being has also shown to have little success. It has been shown that some clients undertaking traditional psychoanalysis get worse, with the remaining numbers either staying the same or improving. Those that improve probably do so because of the 'placebo effect' or because they find a sympathetic listener. But those that feel worse may even falsely attribute their problems to sexual repression or unresolved conflicts between the ego, superego and id. These latter three were concepts that Freud created to explain unresolved conflicts. Fortunately, traditional Freudian theories are rarely used today, although a significantly, modified version of these theories are still practiced by some psychologists in many quarters.

There are of course many schools of psychoanalysis and psychotherapy, each one with its own constructs and system of beliefs. Most of these approaches, unfortunately, have little scientific validity. In other words in most cases do not help patients to resolve their anguish, anxiety or depression over and above the placebo effect. Further, as we have seen above, they may make some of the 'clients' worse and in some instances the client becomes dependent on the therapist with the 'therapy' lasting years.

Timothy B. Baker at the University of Wisconsin has also commented that many psychotherapists fail to "use the interventions for which there is the strongest evidence of efficacy" and "give more weight to their personal experiences than to science".

The reason traditional psychoanalysis still survives is because one third of patients get better no matter what therapy they undertake and of course the psychologists remember these successes. In turn, they falsely attribute these successes to their treatment regimes. It is worth noting that one third of patients get better even if they undertake no therapy.

So what hope is there? Thought control does not seem to work. Traditional psycho- analysis does not have a good track record and positive thinking is not easy.

Fortunately, as you will see in the subsequent chapters there are several approaches and methods that have been scientifically validated, which can help us to change our thinking and embed a more positive and serene outlook so that our past or current situation does not trouble us as much. This, in turn, can help us to improve our well – being, social connectedness and our happiness.

We know intuitively that our thoughts govern our feelings as well as our behavior and that in turn our behavior can affect our thoughts and feelings in a feedback loop.

Shortly we will look at ways to improve our well being using tried and tested methods both from Positive Psychology as well as from Cognitive Behavior Therapy.

But before we do that, we need to look at a few more dubious techniques and understand the placebo effect.

Notes on some other psycho - therapies:
(1) Cognitive Behavior Therapy (CBT) has scientific backing and a good success rate. It has been found helpful in depression, anxiety, obsessive-compulsive disorders, eating disorders, social phobia and post traumatic stress

   Evidence of success: High

(2) Variation on CBT model include: Group Therapy, where the therapist facilitates the group and lets individuals share their problems, challenge each other and discover solutions as a group. This way they can learn from each other. Another aspect of CBT is Couples or Relationship therapies. This has been found to be useful for anorexia nervosa, depression in children and of course for relationship problems. Finally, there is Mindfulness Meditation combined with CBT, that has found to be effective in recurring depression, as well as for some other problems

   Evidence of success: High

(3) Some people do however benefit by other therapies including:
   (a) Psychodynamic Therapies: Significantly revised version of Sigmund Freud's theories. More practical nowadays, the

therapist works with individuals to make sense of their early childhood experiences with their current thoughts, feelings, relationships, dreams and behavior.

Evidence of success: Mixed

(b) Humanistic therapies: These offer an alternative approach to psychodynamic and behavioral therapies. They focus on developing your full potential

Evidence of success: Mixed

(c) Transactional Analysis (TA), pioneered by Eric Berne, looks at repeating scripts that govern our lives as well as our primary modes of conversing, covertly and overtly between Child, Adult and Parent. Sometimes TA is part of humanistic therapies.

Evidence of success: Mixed

(d) Various forms of counseling: Motivational counseling, telephone counseling and life coaching. Some individuals may find these useful for achieving their goals and tackle some emotional issues

Evidence of success: Mixed

Neuro - Linguistic Programming
New Psychology or Mumbo-Jumbo?

The only good is knowledge and the only evil ignorance

Socrates

Chapter 2

Neuro - Linguistic Programming (NLP) - New Psychology or Mumbo Jumbo?

The founding fathers of NLP were Richard Bandler and the linguist John Grinder. There have subsequently been many successful promoters of this 'new psychology', including, Joseph O'Connor and John Seymour. Some of its proponents have called NLP the new learning paradigm and the new language of psychology.

Many techniques have been developed by NLP practitioners, which claim to transform their clients' lives. Anthony Robbins who wrote 'Awaken the Giant Within' and 'Unlimited Power' made this pseudo – science popular. More than eighteen years ago, when I worked for a large International Company, I was one of the management trainers who were sent on a course led by Anthony Robbins to learn the latest rapport building and success building strategies. At this seminar, I was amazed at the psychological high that was built up, often by standing up and affirming 'yes I can'. In some of the exercises we had to visualize our success, yet in others we learnt mirroring techniques, which claimed to build instant and deep rapport. I had mixed feelings after this course; I wasn't sure what to make of it. Many years passed and I revisited NLP literature in order to research some material for this book. Interestingly, I found that despite thin supporting evidence the NLP movement is still going strong, particularly in the corporate world.

Many of the techniques of NLP are intuitively appealing. However, we know that many techniques that appear intuitively correct often fail to give the benefits claimed when they are tested rigorously.

Consider this. We know that to build rapport we need to listen attentively, to paraphrase what we have heard, to nod our heads appropriately and maintain a modicum of eye contact. This helps to demonstrate our understanding as well as show empathy. This is fine and research has shown that this technique does work. However, over the last 30 years, NLP techniques have emerged which claim to build rapport instantly and more deeply. NLP practitioners claim that to build a deeper level of rapport it is necessary to 'mirror' the movements as well as use 'relevant language' of the person you are communicating with. NLP asserts that individuals have Visual, Auditory and Kinesthetic preferences. So for example you might say 'I can see what you are trying to say' to someone who has a visual representation system, as opposed to 'I hear what are getting at' to someone with an auditory style.

However, several research studies have indicated that representational style or system does not seem to play any significant role over and above any active listening method. In other words, active listening by itself it appears is sufficient to build rapport.

Then there is the visualization theme. NLP practitioners claim that to achieve your goals you need to visualize where you want to be.

In fact research has shown that just visualizing in it self will not enable goal realization. Consider the research done by Lien Pham and Shelley Taylor at the University of California. In this study they got a group of students to spend a few moments each day to visualize themselves doing well in their imminent mid-term exams. The control group in this study, were left to carry on normally. The experimenters asked each group to note down how much they studied each day and monitored their final marks. In fact the day - dreaming or visualizing exercise had a negative effect on students' study time. Their behavior made them study less and end up getting lower marks then the control group.

The actual visualization exercise no doubt made them feel good about themselves but there was little success in terms of goal achievement.

In another study Gabriele Oettingen at the University of Pennsylvania monitored students who were aiming to succeed in a career. Oettingen asked her final year students to make a record of how often they dreamed about getting their dream job. When these students were followed up two years later, it was found that the students who visualized their dream job more frequently made fewer applications, received fewer job offers and ended up in less well paid jobs.

It appears that visualizing alone is not enough. In fact, in terms of goal achievement, it may not even be necessary to visualize if there is a plan of action. It appears, as one would expect, that making a plan and acting on it, will significantly help in achieving your goals.

Some NLP practitioners of course have moved on to what works and are quite practical. For example besides just visualizing a goal, they supplement t it with creating a plan of action for the client and then helping them to act on it. So in the case of losing weight, you might visualize yourself as a much slimmer person, create a plan of visiting the gym three times a week and then act on your plan by actually going to the gym. On the other hand some practitioners still practice techniques that have little scientific support. That is they expect 'miracles' just by visualizing the outcome.

NLP has many techniques, including mirroring, anchoring, swishing, re-framing, metaphors and storytelling that include some hypnotic techniques based on the work of Milton Erickson.

As I said earlier, NLP has become very popular in large companies as well as for many distressed individuals. NLP claims amazing successes in treating phobias, OCD, personality disorders, individual growth, rapport building and apparently its ability to inculcate excellent sales and management skills.

Sadly, many of these claims have not been validated. The community of NLP practitioners needs to be more open to clinical trials. When this happens we will then know which techniques work with what success rates. We need to know the outcomes of NLP over and above the placebo effect. Presently, NLP has little if any academic standing. Universities also need to be more receptive to conduct more studies as some techniques may have merit. For many NLP techniques, the jury is still out.

The Placebo Effect
Use Alternative Therapy as a Last Resort

I can believe anything, provided that it is quite incredible
Oscar Wilde

Chapter 3

The Placebo Effect – Use Alternative Therapy as a Last Resort

The placebo effect is well established. It is simply the effect of a dummy pill with no active ingredients that can have a positive effect on some conditions like pain. In fact, any new drug brought out is either compared with a 'sugar pill' as a placebo or an already existing drug to see if it performs better, before releasing it for public consumption.

To put this in historical context, in the early days of clinical trials in the 1950's researchers began using placebos as controls in most clinical studies. Essentially, they would compare the effects of a new drug with a placebo pill that looked exactly the same but had no active ingredient. The placebos established a baseline. The experiments gradually increased in sophistication and were typically 'double blind' meaning that neither the subjects nor the researchers knew who was getting what pills.

Most clinical trials now no longer include 'sugar pill' placebo trials. Instead the controls might include an already existing treatment. This is clearly more ethical and does not invalidate its scientific basis.

But let's go back to the actual placebo effect. How beneficial is it? Is it alright to use the placebo effect for any illness? How can you tap into it?

Research has shown that the placebo effect is real and results in the release of endorphins and other chemicals such as dopamine. It seems that the placebo effect helps in around 30% (sometimes more) of the people, depending on how the dummy pill is administered, the color of the pill, patient expectation and whether a firm diagnosis is made. These are amongst the factors that affect the chances of a placebo effect taking place. It is worth noting that there is no such thing as a placebo personality; it seems we can all be susceptible to it although in a given circumstance different people will respond differently.

Daniel Moerman who has specialized in the placebo effect found that in one study for ulcers the 'placebo' treatment of two sugar pills was compared with placebo trials of four sugar pills. He found, amazingly, that four sugar pills a day are better than two. Incidentally, these trials have been repeated so it's not an isolated finding. We all know that in 'good science' trials have to be repeated.

Here is my own story with homeopathy. About 24 years ago I had a viral infection, which laid me low for many weeks. Although the infection went after 7-10 days, my general malaise and debility persisted for several weeks after. My doctor recommended a whole series of x-rays and blood tests to rule out any underlying problems. Fortunately, all the tests were okay but my extreme fatigue persisted. I was persuaded to visit a homeopath as I felt I had nothing to lose. The homeopath took a detailed history of my symptoms, prescribed me some arnica (a homeopathic remedy), and told me that in a few days I should feel the difference. Surely enough a few days later I was feeling much better, so much so that I went back to work. Something else interesting happened. I also used to suffer from hay-fever in the summer season. It seemed that this homeopathic treatment also helped my hay fever symptoms, totally unrelated to the condition for which I went to see the homeopath in the first place.

I was totally convinced that homeopathy had something going for it. I even rationalized, there was something yet un-discovered, homeopathy may be working at a level we did not yet understand.

How we rationalize things! My belief in homeopathy remained unshaken until a few years later there was a controlled study showing that homeopathic remedies were no better than placebos! I still did not quite believe this as I wondered how my hay fever symptoms also improved. Perhaps this was a badly designed study.

Several years later, a meta-analysis of various studies showed that homeopathy in fact does not have any better outcomes than a placebo.

I also discovered that when a placebo effect is invoked endorphins, amongst other chemicals, are released and indeed these typically help allergies. Clearly, I was helped very significantly by the placebo effect.

Many people claim amazing benefits from homeopathy.

So does this mean we should all visit our homeopaths more often and ask for four sugar pills or arnica pills? The short answer is definitely not. Despite the promising results of placebos, they remain unproven in serious illnesses. Remember for illnesses such as Cancer, TB, Malaria or any other serious illness for that matter conventional drugs work best. And remember the logic, conventional medicines have been tested with placebos, or an existing drug in the first place. They are only available if their effect is significantly better than these. So it makes sense to go for a drug that has a much greater chance of working than a placebo, even if you are worried about the side effects of conventional medicines, as these have usually been factored in.

Recently the World Health Organization has quite rightly warned against the use of homeopathic remedies for Diarrhea, Aids, TB, Malaria and other serious illnesses in the developing world. It seems that some homeopaths are pushing their pills in developing countries for serious illnesses too.

However, if you suffer from pain or another chronic condition, you have already received conventional medicine and are still not improving you may wish to try a safe alternative therapy. In these cases, homeopathy, acupuncture, reflexology, and other therapies may all have their part to play in invoking the placebo effect, and, like me, you could well improve.

It is worth noting that alternative therapy embraces some apparently tried and tested 'herbs' that work. Simon Singh and Edzard Ernst, who have looked at various studies and done a meta- analysis, have some useful information in their book "Trick or treatment? Alternative - Medicine on Trial". If you want to know what really works and what is a placebo as far as alternative therapy is concerned this book is very useful reading.

The Mathematics of a Successful Marriage

The best way to cheer yourself up, is to try to cheer someone else up

Mark Twain

Chapter 4

The Mathematics of a Successful Marriage

We all know that even a little criticism hurts. We know that it can take hours and sometimes days to get over criticism that is hurtful.

On the other hand saying nice things, showing appreciation, being gentle with each other, spending time together can do wonders to maintain or even improve relationships.

My wife wrote a succinct poem that I have re-printed here with her permission, which sums up the importance of being gentle.

The Power of Two

Entwine your hearts and minds
Enmesh your two separate beings
Each one unique and different
But ready to embark
On a journey of togetherness and love

Relationships are strong but fragile
Like eggshells
Be gentle, so gentle

Wrap each other in tendrils of tenderness
And thus armored
Together face
Life's many challenges

In 1994, Dr. John Gottman and his colleagues at the University of Washington made an interesting observation. They found that they could predict with up to 94% accuracy, whether a marriage would end up in divorce.

By observing hundreds of video recordings of conversation between married partners, the researchers were able to formulate with some precision whether a marriage was headed for trouble. What is amazing is that they did this just by observing 15 minutes of interaction. Essentially, the observer counted the number of positive and negative interactions for each couple and then calculated a compatibility ratio. A negative interaction such as showing contempt may count for minus 4 points, whereas showing concern or adding humor to resolve conflict may count for positive two points. These values were number crunched in a special formula and then translated into a probability. This value was the probability of the marriage ending in divorce.

The key finding was the 'five to one' rule. If positive interactions outweigh negative interactions to the said ratio then divorce is very unlikely. In other words, deviations from this ratio increase the likelihood of divorce.

Predicting a divorce outcome may be one thing but sustaining or improving a present relationship is another.

We will see shortly that the Gottmans went on to apply these principles to improving present relationships when needed.

The Gottmans found that there were three types of successful marriages. The validating couple who are good at acknowledging each others problems. They are essentially able to validate each other on their differences and demonstrate empathetic relationships.

Secondly, there is the conflict avoiding couple. This couple tries to avoid hurting each other in the interest of marital stability. They agree to disagree or, at worst, engage in mini fights.

Finally, there is the volatile couple, exactly the opposite of the conflict avoiding couple. In this case they express their emotions vociferously. When they are angry they demonstrate it.

What is interesting is that all styles can lead to a successful marriage providing there is adherence to 'five to one' positive to negative interactions rule.

Their work in their laboratory which was called 'love lab' gave them important clues on how to improve failing but redeemable marriages.

They noticed that many couples in long standing relationships complained of similar things:

'We don't feel close anymore'

'You never talk to me'

'We only have time for the kids'

'You don't care about how I feel'

Most couples face these difficulties.

In their book 'Ten lessons to transform your Marriage' the Gottmans found that when couples addressed key areas of concern even indirectly and applied the five to one rule their relationships usually improved.

Here are the key findings:

Show your concern and be empathetic: whenever your spouse tells you something distressing or troubling, try and put yourself in his or her shoes. Men tend to be less empathetic. So this advice is more applicable to men.

Be less critical of your spouse. The way he washes dinner plates, the way he does various things may be different. Remember one criticism per day will have to be replaced by five pleasantries. So women need to be careful of making small criticisms. As you have probably guessed this form of criticism is more common in women.

Be accepting and tolerant: Accept that there will be differences and try to understand your spouse's point of view. Even if you disagree, see if there is some validity in this other view- point and try to acknowledge this difference.

Listen and show your interest: When your spouse speaks, it is often tempting to interrupt, either by offering a smart answer or finishing the sentence for him or her. Show interest even if you think you know all about it. Demonstrate genuine listening by giving verbal acknowledgements, nods, or direct signaling eye contact.

Be affectionate: You can show affection in ordinary ways through acts of tenderness, touching, holding hands and cuddling.

Show that you care: small acts of thoughtfulness, doing the washing up (if you are husband) or making tea for your spouse are a powerful way to boost the positivity in the ratio of 'five to one'

Be appreciative: Let your spouse know that he or she has done something that pleases you. Acknowledgement helps them feel loved and confident enough to reciprocate.

Argue fairly: When you lose your cool avoid yelling, Explain why you are angry. Successful couples learn how to quickly diffuse anger or to make up shortly after the argument.

Number Crunching rule: Remember the magic of 'five to one'

Also remember to be frequently gentle, so gentle as this approach really does help.

Smiling and Laughter

Sometimes your joy is a source of your smile, but sometimes your smile can be the source of your joy

Thich Nhat Hanh

Chapter 5

Smiling and Laughter

The Facial feed back hypothesis has been demonstrated (Bernstein, et al 2000) in many experiments. In other words whether your face is happy, sad or angry will determine your feelings and vice-versa. In one experiment participants were encouraged to smile by holding a pencil between their teeth. Those who held a pencil between their teeth and thus were able to smile rated the cartoons as funnier than those who held the pencils between their lips and thus could not smile (Davis & Palladino, 2000).

In another experiment persons who were told to make an angry face experienced increased blood flow to their hands and feet, which is what happens when someone is angry. In other experiments persons who were told to smile several times a day for 30 seconds for a week felt happier for several months after.

Research has also found that people who smile in early photos are less likely to be divorced later.

More recently, in February 2009, psychologists at the University of Cardiff found that those who cannot frown because of cosmetic botox injections are happier on average than people who can frown. The researchers had participants fill in questionnaires on anxiety and depression. Around half received frown inhibiting botox injections and the other half received no botox treatment. As expected the botox recipients reported feeling happier and less anxious in general than the control group. The co-author of this study Michael Lewis says 'it would appear that the way we feel our emotions isn't just restricted to our brain –there are parts of our bodies that help and reinforce the feelings we are having. It's like a feedback loop'.

As you may have guessed, the reverse is true as well. In other words frowning makes you feel less happy, but interestingly it can also affect the perception of pain as well. A research study reported in 2008 in the Journal of Pain found that the way pain is felt increases if you are frowning. In this study they applied heat to the forearms of 29 participants, who were asked to make unhappy, neutral or relaxed faces during this procedure. They found that those who were told to exhibit negative expressions such as frowning reported being more in pain than the other two groups. More research is needed to find out if smiling produces even less pain than being neutral or relaxed.

One thing that is certain, however, is that you will be happier if you smile more. Even if you put on a fake smile you will be happier than if you don't.

Here is how you can do it:

Smile as broadly as you can for about 30 seconds

Do this about 3 or 4 times a day

Do this for one week

You should feel happier for several more weeks after this. In other words this simple exercise lasting perhaps two minutes in total every day for seven days can significantly improve your happiness for much longer. It has to be worth a try.

Laughter

We intuitively know that laughter is also good medicine. In 1995 Dr Madan Kataria, a physician from Mumbai came up with a theory that laughter helps to fight depression and stress. He started the so-called laughter yoga clubs, which began to spring up in many parts of the world including the USA and UK. In these classes Laughter Yoga practitioners lead a group of up to 40 people laughing in different ways.

They start with yoga breathing, then move to fake laughter exercises, including roaring like a lion. The theory is that you fake it until you make it. In other words you keep doing these fake laughs until it becomes real.

Participants claim they feel much more energized, invigorated and yes happier.

What however is the evidence? What does science tell us?

It appears that laugher really does have amazing beneficial effects. For example laughter can help in the alleviation of both temporary and chronic pain. This is related to the release of endorphins resulting from laughter (Cinciripani & Floreen 1983). Further benefits include the alleviation of stress and anxiety. This is why many health clinics now offer different forms of laughter therapy for these stress related conditions. In addition, linked to stress reduction it has also been found to have a beneficial effect on blood pressure and heart rate (McMahon et al, 2005), although during the actual act of laughing, blood pressure, can rise a bit. Laughter it appears also boosts the immune system. The number of T-cells and the production of antibodies both increase.

However, like any good medicine you need to be careful not too exert your tummy muscles too much whilst laughing in particular be careful if you are asthmatic (as vigorous laughter may trigger asthmatic attacks), or if you have recently had abdominal surgery. But if you are otherwise well a little laughter every day will do you a world of good. And if you want to avoid laughing make sure you smile!

Increasing your Happiness - Initial Thoughts

Man is fond of counting his troubles, but he does not count his joys. If he counted them, as he ought to, he would see that every lot has enough provided for it

Fyodor Dostoevsky

Chapter 6

Increasing your Happiness - Initial Thoughts

Happiness is what we all intuitively want and yet sometimes it seems to be elusive to get. Sonja Lyubomirsky and her colleagues at University of California researched thousands of men and women in various happiness studies. What they found was impressive. It appears that cultivating happiness makes people more sociable and more compassionate. It increases their own self- esteem as well as their regard for other people. It helps them to have more satisfying relationships and be more successful in their careers.

The same cohorts also seem to have a stronger immune system and live longer. Clearly our desire to be happy is well founded. But can we achieve this elusive state of happiness? Various twin-based studies have shown that approximately 50% of our happiness is set at birth, another 10% is due to circumstances and environment, but 40% (a significant portion) is within our control. For example, a study done by behavior geneticists David Lykken, Auke Tellegen et al has shown that the variation in total happiness amongst identical twins is much less than with fraternal twins or siblings. This suggests a higher correlation in base levels of happiness with identical twins whether raised together or apart. However, what is interesting is that amongst fraternal twins or siblings the levels of happiness seem totally uncorrelated. In other words, what your life outcomes are or what you do with your life can significantly increase or decrease your happiness.

A small percentage of people, who are lucky to be endowed with a high happiness set-point will naturally experience high levels of energy, enthusiasm and well being. However, for most of us with average or even below average set points of happiness it is reassuring to know that we can change our overall levels more favorably.

A significant amount of research shows that individuals adjust to a wide range of circumstances; for example, paraplegics revert to their original happiness levels, with many scoring positively on happiness scores within a year of their spinal cord injuries. Conversely, lottery winners, after their initial spike in happiness, quickly settle back to their normal scores. Newly weds lose their initial euphoria and settle down with normal ups and downs of life. Additional pay rises at work soon wear off in terms of their happiness lift, or, for that matter, any big purchase that you make gives you an initial boost in happiness only to wear off in a short time.

On a more optimistic note, in terms of measuring happiness, it seems most of us are at least mildly happy. Studies have been done in dozens of countries showing similar results. However, being mildly happy is obviously not the same as being moderately happy, happy or very happy.

The question then arises whether it is possible for most of us to increase our happiness to higher levels? In other words, if we are mildly or moderately happy can we become happy or very happy? And in the unfortunate instance that we are unhappy or very unhappy can we become at least moderately happy?

It appears that there are several tried and tested techniques that can boost our happiness levels significantly but, like most things in life, we have to practice these skills in order to benefit from them. However, when they become second nature, research shows we are better able to cope with many of the stresses that life presents us with. In turn, we benefit with more frequent experiences of joy, energy, enthusiasm and well–being.

We will now look at some techniques that can increase our happiness:

Being Grateful

Religions as well as many philosophies have long established the value of gratitude in adding to one's well - being and happiness. However, it is relatively recently that science has been able to validate the role gratitude plays in one's happiness as well as health. Consider some research done by Emmons & McCullough at the University of Miami. Here are some of their findings:

Those who kept gratitude journals on a weekly basis exercised more regularly, felt better about their lives as a whole, and were generally more optimistic about the upcoming week compared to the experimental group who recorded hassles or neutral life events. In addition, there appeared to be personal benefit in the realm of goal attainment. It was found that persons who kept gratitude lists were more likely to achieve their goals (academic, interpersonal and health based) over a two-month period compared to subjects in other experimental conditions.

The same gratitude intervention in young adults resulted in higher levels of alertness, enthusiasm, attentiveness and energy compared to those who focused on hassles or downward social comparisons (e.g. I am worse off than him)

In a sample of adults with neuromuscular disease a three- week gratitude intervention resulted in greater levels of positive moods, a greater sense of connectedness to others, and better sleep quality compared to a control group

In summary, 'grateful people' report higher levels of positive emotions, life satisfaction, and energy, and are generally more optimistic. Conversely, they seem to have lower levels of depression and stress.

So what can you do to increase your levels of gratefulness?

First and foremost, keep a gratitude diary or journal. Every week write down five to ten things for which you are grateful. These can be really small things like you had a nice lunch on Monday, the weather was great on Tuesday, in the evening it was so nice to be with family and so on. Start with whatever grateful thought springs to mind. Do not worry if you cannot think of any major events. Do this activity once a week for six weeks and see how you feel. You may be pleasantly surprised at your newfound well - being. You do not have to do this gratitude exercise every day. Sonja Lyubominsky in her book 'The How of Happiness' researched that doing a gratitude journal everyday could become boring and may lose its power. It may be better to do the gratitude list weekly as suggested and also to vary it week by week. Try to find different things for which you are grateful every week.

There are, of course, other techniques to improve your happiness. Let us look at some research done by Barbara Fredrickson which shows that what makes us happy and resilient is not so much the lack of negative feelings but the balance of positive to negative experiences. It turns out that if you have at least three positive emotions for every one negative emotion you are going to be happy.

This research has also shown that appropriate negative feelings are not only beneficial but necessary to the human psyche. For example, it is appropriate to grieve or be sad at a funeral, to be angry when you lose your job, to feel hurt when some one is scornful, to be sad at the sight of poverty. These negative feelings hopefully mobilize us into action. They help us to empathize with our grieving friends or relatives, to apply for more jobs when we lose our own job, to deal with anger by letting someone know that what they said was not appropriate and, of course, in the case of poverty to mobilize us into action by giving. It is only when negative feelings arising from our distorted self perceptions, anxieties and lack of self-esteem take over our positive emotional experiences that we tend to go downward in a negative spiral and perhaps depression.

We know from Gottman's observations on successful marriages that criticism has much more impact than a pleasantry. Remember, for a successful relationship the ratio of pleasantries to criticism was 5:1 Similarly, for personal happiness and well-being a negative emotion has a more lasting effect than a positive emotion. Thus, Barbara Fredrickson advocates developing strategies for increasing your ratio of positive and negative emotions to 3:1, in order to be happy. This is backed by extensive research. Her 'Broaden and Build' theory asserts that you can increase your reservoir of happiness by having the positive and negative emotions operate in the ratio of 3:1 or better. The idea is not to remove negative emotions altogether but rather to improve the ratio of positive to negative emotions in the appropriate ratio.

In fact, Barbara Fredrickson has identified 10 types of positive emotions that can play a role in increasing your happiness.

(1) Amused, fun loving or silly

(2) Awed, wonder or amazement

(3) Grateful, appreciative or thankful

(4) Hopeful, optimistic or encouraged

(5) Inspired, uplifted or elevated

(6) Interested, alert or curious

(7) Joyful, glad or happy

(8) Love, closeness or trust

(9) Proud, confident or self assured

(10) Serene, content or peaceful

So how can you use this list? You can 'broaden and build' your happiness and resilience by practicing more positive emotions from a few of those given in the list. This could involve doing small things regularly that increase your positive experiences. For example, being regularly grateful is obviously one powerful method. You can read an inspiring novel or watch an engaging movie, you can go out and eat with your friend or partner, you can join a group (e.g. yoga, tai-chi, bridge-club, reading-club or dancing). You can try to cultivate more serenity through meditation. You can be more appreciative, optimistic, fun loving and silly. You can take long walks or exercise regularly and you can smile more. You can be more absorbed by undertaking something you enjoy. The list is endless. However, putting these ideas into action may not be as easy as the list suggests. Later on in this book we will be dealing with a few specific techniques to help us build this repertoire in order to enable us to enter an upward spiral in experiencing more joy and happiness.

Meanwhile you may want to research Barbara Fredrickson's website and measure your own positivity ratio: www.positivityratio.com

We saw in the first chapter that, until recently, from Freud onwards psychologists have been concentrating on finding out what is wrong with us. They did this by dwelling on our childhood traumas and experiences in order to untangle our emotional conflicts. In other words, they have been concentrating on models that can help us to revert back to 'normal'. We have seen in the first chapter that many of these earlier psychological models were in fact ineffective.

Fortunately, Cognitive Behavior Therapy (CBT), which we will look at later, has largely replaced traditional psychoanalysis and put psychology on a more scientific footing.

Recently however, Positive Psychology, also based on scientific findings, is beginning to concentrate on increasing our happiness rather than just making us normal or average or, for that matter on focusing on just 'removing' a problem.

According to Martin Seligman, positive psychology encourages us to increase our positive experiences such as kindness, humor, gratitude and appreciation. This, he claims, is a better way to dissolve our mental distress, depression and despair. In addition, for the 'normal' individual, like the majority of us, positive psychology can help us lead a more fulfilling and joyous life.

Martin Seligman further recommends that you identify your strongest five signature strengths from the twenty-four that he has identified. In turn if you can incorporate these five signature strengths into your daily life activities, such as work and personal life, you will be 'authentically happy'.

As mentioned earlier, in the ensuing chapters we will look at some specific techniques that research shows are highly likely to increase your happiness.

If you intend to embark on experimenting with increasing your happiness you may want to first find out what your base line level is.

For interest and cross validation, another short questionnaire is also provided later. This is the Life Satisfaction questionnaire devised by Dr. Ed Diener

The Oxford Happiness Questionnaire

(Developed by Michael Argyle & Peter Hills at Oxford University, (2002)

This questionnaire has been validated as being relatively stable and accurate and it is a good way to get a snapshot of your current level of happiness. If you embark on some of the happiness exercises listed in this book your happiness level should increase. You can validate this by re- taking this test in another month's time.

Instructions

Below are a number of statements about happiness. Please indicate how much you agree or disagree with each by entering a number in the blank after each statement, according to the following scale:

1 = strongly disagree

2= moderately disagree

3 = slightly disagree

4 = slightly agree

5 = moderately agree

6 = strongly agree

Please read the statements carefully and answer without too much hesitation.

1. I do not feel particularly pleased with the way I am (X) _____
2. I am intensely interested in other people _____
3. I feel that life is very rewarding _____
4. I have very warm feelings towards almost everyone _____
5. I rarely wake up feeling rested (X) _____
6. I am not particularly optimistic about the future (X) _____
7. I Find most things amusing _____
8. I am always committed and involved _____
9. Life is good _____
10. I do not think the world is a good place (X) _____
11. I laugh a lot _____
12. I am well satisfied with everything in my life _____
13. I do not think I look attractive (X) _____
14. There is a gap between what I would like to do and what I have done (X)_____
15. I am very happy _____
16. I find beauty in some things _____
17. I always have a cheerful effect on others _____
18. I can fit in everything I want to _____
19. I feel that I am not especially in control of my life (X) _____
20. I feel able to take on anything _____
21. I feel fully mentally alert _____
22. I often experience joy and elation _____
23. I do not find it easy to make decisions (X) _____
24. I do not have a particular sense of meaning and purpose in my life (X) _____
25. I feel I have a great deal of energy _____
26. I usually have a good influence on events _____

27. I do not have fun with other people (X) _____

28. I do not feel particularly healthy (X) _____

29. I do not have particularly happy memories of the past (X) _____

Calculate your score

Step 1: The items marked X should be scored in reverse:

If you gave yourself a "1", cross it out and change it to "6"

Similarly, Change "2" to a "5"

Change "3" to a "4"

Change "4 to a "3"

Change "5" to a "2"

Change "6" to a "1"

Step 2: Having made the appropriate changes add all the numbers for all 29 questions

Step3: Divide the total by 29

Note the score and date it. Try and repeat this periodically to note any changes.

The lowest possible score is 1 and the highest is 6. It seems the average score is 4.3

You can see what your own score is and how it improves over a period of time as you undertake some of these activities

You may now like to take another happiness questionnaire, devised by Dr. Diener

Satisfaction with Life Scale (devised by Ed Diener)

For each of the statements below, put a value between 1 and 7 depending on how much you agree or disagree with it.

Use the following point scale:

7 – Strongly agree

6 – Agree

5 – Slightly agree

4 – Neither agree nor disagree

3 – Slightly disagree

2 – Disagree

1 – Strongly disagree

    (1) In most ways my life is close to my ideal _____

    (2) The conditions of my life are excellent _____

    (3) I am satisfied with my life _____

    (4) So far I've gotten the important things I want in life _____

    (5) If I could live my life over, I would change almost nothing __

Add all the numbers you wrote besides each question. Compare your total to the descriptions below.

31 – 35 Extremely Satisfied

26 – 30 Satisfied

21 – 25 Slightly Satisfied

20 – Neutral

15 –19 Slightly Dissatisfied

10 – 14 Dissatisfied

5 – 9 Extremely Dissatisfied

Optimism

When you have seven percent unemployed, you have ninety-three percent working

John F. Kennedy

Chapter 7

Optimism

Yes, you have guessed right. Optimism is good for you. Optimists have less illness and recover more quickly than pessimists. Optimists are happier and healthier and have an actuarially longer life. This does not mean that next time you are ill you should just rely on optimism and not consult your doctor or stop taking your medication. However, being optimistic will aid your recovery. Consider the famous nun study done on the autobiographical content of their final vows before they entered the convent in 1900. The researchers found that 90% of the nuns in the top 25% who wrote the most optimistic notes were still alive at age 84. In contrast, only 34% of the least positive quarter were still alive. What is even more interesting is that more than 50% of this positive quarter, were still alive at 94.

In another study at the Mayo clinic in the US researchers administered various tests, including a test on optimism, on 900 people who referred themselves for medical care. The researchers followed up these patients and observed that 30 years later the optimists lived nearly 20% longer than the pessimists.

Optimists tend to achieve more and appear to have more than their fair share of luck. Further research shows it is their persistence and resilience that makes for this difference in success. Optimists are specially successful in sales and marketing.

In a particular study, Martin Seligman worked with the Metropolitan Life Insurance Company and studied their agents' success rates with optimism. In 1985, 15,000 applicants took both an attributional style questionnaire (measuring optimism) and Met Life's career profile. One thousand agents were hired based solely on their own career profile as Met Life had done in the past. However, since Met Life had a chronic shortage of agents they also hired an additional 100 agents who scored just below the cut off point of their own career profile but who were in the top half of the optimism related questionnaire. After two years, the optimists in the regular group of hires were outselling the pessimists by 31%. Amazingly, however, the 100 additional agents hired outsold the pessimists in the regular force by 57%.

What is optimism? How do optimists think? Is it always beneficial to be an optimist?

Optimists consider negative events as temporary; they do not personalize the event but attribute it to a particular set of circumstances and move on.

Pessimists, on the other hand, consider negative events or setbacks as permanent (it will always be like this). Further they view this setback as a personal failure (it always happens to me) and generalize (all events seem to turn out like this)

Seligman believes that there is a causal link between pessimism and depression, which is controversial. Some studies have shown a genetic link to depression although this, like the happiness set point can be changed a fair amount. However, if a person learns to be more optimistic there is empirical evidence to show that they will gradually lift themselves out of depression and be much happier as a result.

Although we have seen the many benefits of optimism it is worth pointing out one main disadvantage. Too much optimism can lead to Pollyanna type behavior where one's judgment may be clouded and excessive risk taking behavior can occur. This has been particularly evident in the financial sector where sub-prime mortgage lending became disproportional and Ninja (no income, no job or assets) loans also became popular. No doubt this type of collective group optimism by bankers was one of the main reasons for the recent financial crisis.

However, optimism is advantageous if it is balanced and realistic but not extreme. Pessimists, in contrast, are generally risk-averse and are valuable to have in a professional setting, in tasks where a more accurate risk assessment is needed. Realistic optimism is what we should aim for. This type of optimism can help us be more adventurous without taking undue risks, helps us be healthier and prevents us from sinking into despair and depression.

So how do we become more realistically optimistic?

When faced with a setback or challenge make a note of how you react. Write down your thinking & feelings. It might go something like this: 'This always happens to me', "It must be my fault', 'I can't see things improving, I'm sure this will happen again'. Once you have recorded it, ask yourself how you felt. Perhaps you felt low or found yourself ruminating.

The next task is to challenge the thoughts that you have written down and re-write what it could have been. E.g. 'this setback happened because of very special circumstances', 'It wasn't completely my fault', 'it may not happen again'.

Now the next time you have a setback try and recall what you wrote down and practice the 'alternative,' more realistic optimistic thoughts. It may just work wonders for you.

Prayer and Compassion

If you want others to be happy practice compassion. If you want to be happy practice compassion

Dalai Lama

Chapter 8

Prayer and Compassion

Neal Krause from the University of Michigan conducted some research on prayers. One of his studies focused on the elderly population to investigate if prayer could support their health. Interestingly he found that praying for improvement in their own lives for material things such as more money, a better car or a better house offered no increase in happiness or well-being, whereas prayers for others (compassion) increased the praying individual's well being. Praying for others also improved the others well being provided they were told that they were being prayed for. This was probably, because they felt loved and cared for.

Based on more than a 1000 interviews, Krause found that praying for others helped them (the praying individuals) to reduce their stress level, increase their happiness as well reduce symptoms from any ill health they themselves may have been suffering.

In all religious traditions prayer and compassion is recommended. For example, Buddhist traditions have long emphasized the importance of cultivating connection and practicing 'loving kindness meditation' (LKM). In fact, the Dalai Lama has spent most of his life telling us the importance of LKM as a means of enhancing individual happiness as well as our social connectedness. This refers to increasing trust, co-operation and empathy with the individuals you interact with.

Is there more evidence that this kind of compassion meditation, that is LKM, helps one's well being? How compelling is the evidence for us to practice this? What is LKM? Finally, how does one practice LKM?

One study done at Stanford University by Cendri A. Hutcherson et al was to test the hypothesis that 'Loving-Kindness Meditation' increased social connectedness and happiness. To assess this, they examined its effect on positive and negative mood both before starting and at the end of these LKM exercises. Two groups were taken, the LKM condition and the IMAGERY condition. The latter was designed to be as structurally similar as possible to LKM instructions while remaining affectively neutral. Both groups began with instructions to close their eyes, relax and take deep breaths. However, what followed changed. The LKM group (a sample of 45 persons) were instructed to imagine two loved ones standing on either side of the participant and sending their love.

After four minutes participants were told to open their eyes and re-direct these feelings of love and compassion towards a photograph of a neutral stranger appearing at the center of the screen.

Participants then repeated a series of phrases designed to bring attention to the other, to wish them health, happiness and well - being. This is a kind of compassion prayer.

In the IMAGERY condition (a sample of 48 persons) the original relaxation exercise was followed by different instructions. They were asked to imagine two acquaintances they did not know very well and for whom they did not have any strong feelings standing to either side of them. Participants were told to focus on each acquaintance's physical appearance. After 4 minutes the participants were told to open their eyes, look at a photograph of a neutral stranger and focus their attention on the visual details of the stranger's face and appearance. Remember there were two groups, the LKM and the IMAGERY control group. For both groups a second set of measures of mood followed the exercises. The results demonstrated with a high level of statistical significance that the participants in the LKM group were more positive as measured by calmness, happiness and lovingness as opposed to anger, anxiousness and unhappiness.

More research by Fredrickson et al at the University of North Carolina in 2001 worked on the hypothesis of 'broaden and build' theory of positive emotions and compassion. This asserts that people's daily experiences of positive emotions compound over time to build a variety of personal resources. That is to say they become more socially engaged, more mindful, less stressed and generally have decreased illness symptoms. This, in turn, increases their life satisfaction and happiness and reduces their depressive symptoms. This build hypothesis was tested in a field experiment with working adults, a sample of 139 participants. Approximately half were randomly assigned to practice either LKM or neutral. The results indeed showed that over a period of time the LKM group produced increases of the kind predicted. In other words it made the participants more resilient.

Dacher Keltner, at the University of California in Berkeley, in his recent book, Born to be Good, claims that during acts of kindness, generosity and self-sacrifice the vagus nerve is activated, which in turn reduces the heart rate and generates a feeling of warm expansion in the chest. Keltner believes that these 'compassionate feelings' helps us to connect to one another, to care for each other, to help bond and live co-operatively in groups. This type of response, he believes, is genetically built in and serves an evolutionary purpose.

Let us look at another more practical reason why compassionate training may help. Some studies done by Professor Paul Gilbert has found that training in compassion building exercises helps individuals to reduce self- criticism.

Professor Paul Gilbert (author of the 'Compassionate Mind') finds that shame and high levels of self-criticism occur in a variety of difficulties, including social anxiety, eating disorders and some other personality difficulties. He has developed a version of LKM called Compassionate Focused Therapy in which the first task is for individuals to start accepting themselves 'non-judgmentally'. They are then trained to be more compassionate to themselves and others as well as to challenge some of their thinking. These studies show that, over a period of time, a significant proportion of participants with these types of problems respond favorably. In other words, individuals become less critical towards themselves and more positive about life. They feel less shame and feel socially less anxious, or their eating disorder recedes.

We have seen that there are many studies that demonstrate the benefits of being more compassionate. We have seen that this, in turn, helps us not only to improve our own well- being but, in fact, aids us to become more meaningfully engaged and help others.

So how do we practice LKM?

Step 1

The first important step is to simply be aware of your thoughts. What do you normally think of when you feel low? If you feel self-critical and full of shame just be aware that that these are your thoughts you are experiencing - do not judge them as good or bad, simply be aware that the low feelings you have are resulting from this thinking, which unfortunately is automatic. This last bit is important; the thoughts you are having are automatic and at present you have little control over them.

Step 2

Once you realize that the thoughts are automatic and this need not always be the case you can then try step 3. This is easier said than done but keep reflecting on this process that at present you have little control over your thoughts but soon you are going to try and change this pattern of thinking with established and scientifically proven techniques.

Step 3

To practice LKM you can close your eyes, take a few deep breaths, relax as much as you can and think of someone you like (a friend, a partner, or someone from your family) and send them kind thoughts and wishes, 'I wish him/her good health, happiness and well- being. I wish him/her freedom from pain and suffering and may he/she experience joy. Repeat this for all your family members, any friends, acquaintances or even people you admire but have not met. Now repeat this for someone you feel neutral about and finally repeat this for someone you don't like.

Step 4.

We now come to the most important part. You need to now practice LKM on yourself. 'May I be free from self pity and self criticism, may I experience joy and happiness, may I experience love and well being'.

You might find this last part difficult, but it is important to go through these or similar statements.

Every day or even every few days if need be go through these 4 steps for a few minutes a day.

Remember, whatever your beliefs compassion training works. It appears that we have an evolutionary need to be compassionate as this leads to a sense of social connectedness and co-operation which are key components of group as well as individual well being. Being kind, compassionate and caring is, of course, part of the virtues tradition preached by moral philosophy as well as all major religions.

Although you do not have to be religious to be 'compassionate' it seems that having faith increases the likelihood of 'compassionate' behavior.

You may also be interested in combining LKM with Mindfulness training. We will explore Mindfulness Training in the next chapter.

Mindfulness Meditation

The happiness that is genuinely satisfying is accompanied by the fullest exercise of our faculties and the fullest realization of the world we live in

Bertrand Russell

Chapter 9

Mindfulness Meditation

We have seen from the first chapter that it is difficult to control one's thinking. We have seen that we cannot just stop worrying or suppress unwanted thoughts. Thoughts, it appears, have their own mode of operating. Our minds tend to wander and jump from one thing to another. We have also seen that our thoughts influence our feelings and vice versa. We need some methods or techniques to distract ourselves from these unwanted thoughts so that we can be free from unnecessary worry and stress.

One such technique that has gained popularity in recent years is that of mindfulness meditation. It appears that meditation has a very relaxing and positive effect on your well-being. Research results show that participants who meditate regularly feel happier, more peaceful, more energetic and even healthier than those who don't. In turn, individuals who meditate are less pre-occupied with their troublesome thoughts.

So, what exactly are the benefits and what research has been done to convince us that this is, in fact, the case?

Finally, how does one practice mindfulness meditation?

Although a significant amount of research has been done on the benefits of mindfulness meditation in the last 20 years, unfortunately many studies were badly designed with no control groups or their equivalent. We have seen from the chapter on the 'placebo effect' that unless the design of the study has a scientific basis then its results are open to question or even suspect. Fortunately, in the last few years several specific studies with control groups have been done. The results have been quite impressive.

Much of the research done is due to the pioneering efforts of Jon Kabat-Zinn with his Mindfulness Based Stress Reduction (MBSR) training program. We will now look at some good studies from the past as well as those of a more recent origin.

One of the earliest studies done by Jon Kabat-Zinn, Wheeler, et al in 1998 was a clinical trial with patients with severe psoriasis. This study found that patients with severe psoriasis undergoing photo-therapy and listening to guided meditation tapes while receiving the ultra-violet light treatment healed at approximately four times the rate of subjects receiving just the light treatment. Later, this observation of an increased rate of skin clearing amongst meditators was repeated in another study with a better control group.

There have also been many consistent, reliable and reproducible results that demonstrate that MBSR helps in lowering blood pressure, decreases stress, increases happiness and well-being as well as having a positive effect on the immune system.

Consider a study done by Richard Davidson, Jon Kabat-Zinn, et al in 2002 on brain changes for meditators versus non-meditators. This study found that a short program of mindfulness meditation produced a noticeable effect on the brain and immune function. In other words meditators had improved cognitive functions and experienced a sense of well - being. Similar research has been repeated at Harvard, Yale and the Massachusetts Institute of Technology on long- term meditators. Brain scans revealed that experienced meditators had increased thickness in parts of their brains that deal with attention and processing sensory input. Further studies were done on experienced meditators by neuroscientist Richard Davidson. He found that long-term meditation has a profound and permanent impact on the brain, improving its capacity for awareness and happiness. This study found that experienced meditators show high-frequency gamma waves associated with higher mental activity, perception, consciousness and happiness.

Based on Jon Kabat-Zinn's work, Zindel Segal, Mark Williams and John Teasdale adapted the MBSR program so it could be used for people who had suffered from repeated episodes of depression in their lives. Their modified methodology, called Mindfulness Based Cognitive therapy, has been so successful that the National Institute of Clinical Excellence (NICE), in the UK has recommended it as an effective treatment for the relapse of depression. Research has shown that people who have been depressed three or more times for many years can significantly reduce their chances of depression returning by practicing mindfulness meditation.

But what is fascinating is that most individuals who are just ordinarily stressed out with every day life problems can significantly increase their well -being and happiness too. Just as in the last chapter we saw the benefits of Loving Kindness Meditation, here we can see the benefits of mindfulness training.

So how do we practice mindfulness meditation?

To help us practice formally it is important first to remember some key principles.

Thoughts are just thoughts – do not identify yourself with your thoughts

> (1) If you become aware of your thoughts simply accept them as your thoughts; do this non- judgmentally whatever they are. In other words, befriend your thoughts, and paradoxically troublesome thoughts begin to lose their impact
>
> (2) To formalize this process begin to be aware of the moment, starting with your breath

Formal Practice:

> (1) Sit down upright in a comfortable position on a chair or a cushion
>
> (2) Try and let go of tension in your face, shoulders, neck, arms and the rest of your body
>
> (3) Breathe normally and just watch your breath
>
> (4) Gradually close your eyes (if you haven't already) and keep watching your breath going in and out
>
> (5) As you find your mind wandering, accept your current thinking and refocus on your breath
>
> (6) Keep repeating this process, watching your breath flowing gently in and out of your nostrils and befriending your thoughts when your mind wanders

This process is simple yet many find it difficult to do initially. In the early stages of meditation practice when 'thoughts' intrude the aspiring meditator thinks, 'Oh I must be doing this incorrectly, I cannot seem to focus on my breathing'. Remember not to blame yourself but simply to accept your thoughts. Let's suppose you are meditating and you think about the argument you recently had, or what you will have for lunch or what you have to do to day, simply say 'that's interesting, I have just been thinking about my lunch. I will now go back and watch my breath. Keep re-directing your attention to your breathing. When you notice your thoughts and feelings or external sounds occur simply accept them, notice them, do not judge them and redirect your attention to your breath. Remember it's natural for thoughts and feelings to arise and even for you to often get involved with them. The trick is to return to your breath as often as necessary without being angry.

Practice this simple process for 5 to10 minutes every day, gradually increasing it to 20 minutes everyday. Do not expect an immediate transformation or a sense of well - being. This rarely happens. The process may be quite boring initially and 5 minutes may seem endless, but keep at it. You will be amazed at your new- found tranquility after a few weeks of this practice. Remember, like any exercise, you need to do it regularly for several weeks before you see the benefits.

Many individuals practicing this non-judgmental form of mindfulness meditation have improved their quality of life significantly. They feel more happy less anxious, more relaxed, more socially connected, more compassionate and less troubled by their previously troublesome thoughts.

In this respect mindfulness meditation training is more akin to the new form of therapy called acceptance and commitment therapy (ACT) rather than cognitive behavior therapy (CBT). It appears that one method of diffusing troublesome thoughts is simply to accept them. In the case of negative feelings emerging just accept these non-judgmentally without necessarily challenging them. Simply observe the thoughts without identifying with them.

So, for example, if the thought 'I am no good' enters your mind, you simply say to yourself "that's interesting. I notice that I had this persistent thought that 'I am no good' – also I noticed that I became engaged with the thought. I will now return to watching my breath."

Once you learn to detach yourself from the thought and become the observer then gradually the thought seems to lose its power. This is the so- called diffusion effect in ACT jargon.

Try and practice mindfulness on an informal basis too. You can do this by being more aware of the moment. When eating, eat slowly and enjoy your food. When you have a shower notice the pleasant feeling of the water on the different parts of your body, when in the garden observe the flowers and trees, when walking enjoy your walk and even when undertaking mundane tasks be aware of them as non-judgmentally as possible. You can also incorporate small intervals of time for mindfulness meditation. For example, when starting the day, watch your breath going in and out just for one minute. Repeat this the last thing at night. Once you become experienced at being more engaged with your moment- to- moment activities a new level of peace and equanimity will pervade your life.

Does this mean you will just be happy in a delusional sense and not be in touch with your own difficulties? On the contrary, it appears that mindfulness training helps you become more engaged with the world here and now. It helps you to be more productive, more proactive with your real problems. Finally, it helps you to be more energetic, more compassionate and more- happy so that you can be more useful to yourself and others.

Some studies have also shown that mindfulness meditation can be useful for Attention Deficit Hyperactivity Disorder (ADHD), sometimes called Attention Deficit Disorder (ADD). ADD can be disconcerting at all ages and is often unrecognized in adults. The reason for this is that many adults function 'normally' but have great problems in their ability to focus or maintain attention.

Fortunately, ADD can be helped by both behavior therapy as well as drugs. But recently mindfulness training has also been found to be of significant help in tackling this problem. Consider the study done by Dr. David Rabiner at the Department of Psychology and Neuroscience at Duke University.

Dr David Rabiner studied 24 adults and 8 adolescents who were diagnosed with ADHD. About two thirds were already being treated with stimulant medication. The majority of adults had also struggled with various psychiatric and mood disorders. Mindfulness meditation was prescribed as described above. In other words, they were asked to focus on their breathing and whenever their mind wandered they had to bring their awareness back to their breathing. This mindfulness-training program lasted for 8 weeks. Each home training session was recommended to be 45 minutes. On average the participants completed 2.5 hours of meditation per week, much shorter than that prescribed. Various psychological pre- and post- tests took place. The results were very impressive. 78 percent of participants reported a reduction in their ADHD symptoms. In the case of those already taking medication, they experienced even further reduction in their symptoms. In addition, many participants reported improvements in their mood and psychiatric symptoms.

It is not surprising that meditation works. Individuals with ADD suffer from self-regulation problems. In other words, they have problems in maintaining their attention or focus, controlling hyperactivity and managing impulses.

Mindfulness meditation helps in training individuals to be more focused. Gradually, the ability to maintain attention improves. We have also seen that meditation helps improve mood and enhances well-being. These feelings in turn help to increase an individual's self esteem.

It would be silly to say that the first course of treatment for ADHD/ADD is to try meditation. But it certainly seems another approach or a complementary approach to drug and behavior therapy.

Here we have discussed the benefits of mindfulness training. It appears that any form of meditation that requires focusing, for example repeating a mantra such as 'om' as in the Hindu tradition or doing Zikr as in the Sufi tradition, or indeed focusing on a candle or on any object as in the yoga tradition will work just as well.

There is another type of non-faith based meditation worth mentioning.

Dr. Herbert Benson at the Harvard Medical School more than twenty five years ago showed that simply repeating any neutral word like 'one' for 15 to 20 minutes twice a day can induce what he termed the 'relaxation response'. This form of meditation is very similar to a mantra type meditation that is popular with transcendental meditation (TM.). However, Herbert Benson in his more recent book 'Beyond The Relaxation Response' identifies yet another factor that helps meditation even more. His observations lead him to the conclusion that meditation combined with 'faith,' be it religious or philosophical, leads to even better outcomes for happiness and well –being.

However, suffice it to say, that many studies with appropriate control groups have demonstrated that simply repeating a word such as 'one' for several minutes, even without faith can be beneficial in reducing stress and increasing well- being including helping anxiety, sleeplessness, headaches and other stress related problems.

On a practical level, some people find 'concentration' types of meditation more difficult. More training and practice than mindfulness meditation may be required. Here we have looked at the easier option of practicing 'mindfulness meditation'. Needless to say, you need to choose the type of meditation that you feel most comfortable with.

Finally, as I said before, for meditation to work you do not have to be religious. It works well for atheists, agnostics, humanists, and of course for religious people too!

Punching Pillows Does Not Quell Your Anger

Holding on to anger is like grasping a hot coal with the intent of throwing it at someone else; you are the one that gets burned

Buddha

Chapter 10

Punching Pillows Does not Quell Your Anger

We know that anger can make us very stressed and sometimes even ill. In the last fifteen years there have been many studies showing that emotions such as anger and hostility are detrimental to our health.

Dr. Redford Williams at Duke University and Dr. Robert Sapolsky at Stanford University have independently demonstrated in their studies that anger, rage and hostility can be very damaging to our heart health. In fact studies have shown that anger is a major independent risk factor as high as conventional risk factors like high blood cholesterol and high blood pressure in Coronary Heart Disease. So, given the damaging effects of anger, how do we manage it?

Many psychologists have recommended the 'cathartic' approach for anger management. Essentially the theory asserts that, if you punch bags, shout and scream when you are angry you should displace your frustration and feel better. This approach has gained wide acceptance and still practiced by many 'life coaches' and 'anger management' specialists. Unfortunately, this intuitively appealing theory has little scientific basis and has recently been shown not to work.

Consider the research done by Brad Bushmen from Iowa State University. In this experiment students were artificially made to feel frustrated and angry by purposely being given low marks as well as negative feedback in one of their assignments. At the outset the students obviously did not know the game plan. After they received the negative feedback and wrongly assessed low mark, some students were given the opportunity to vent their feelings. They were given a pair of boxing gloves and told to hit a punch bag. Another group of the same cohort were asked to sit in a quiet room for 2 minutes. Questionnaires were completed at the end of the experiment for both groups where various mood categories including how angry they felt were recorded. Interestingly, the results revealed that the group that had punched bags felt significantly more aggressive afterwards. Further, their negative mood persisted for a much longer time. This study has been repeated several times with the same results.

So, if punching a bag doesn't quell your anger what can help?

Fortunately, there are several well-known techniques that do work.

But before we look at this list of techniques that work it is worth pointing out the results of a study done by Michael McCullough et al at the University of Miami.

McCullough found, paradoxically, that if you spend a few minutes focusing on the benefits gained from what appeared to be a hurtful and anger provoking experience then this generally helps you to reduce your frustration and makes you calmer. Now, finding benefits from negative life experiences is not easy, but by turning to a different perspective and trying to see what you have learnt from this experience can help. So the next time, you become angry try seeing what you can learn from this experience. You may realize, for example, that may be the person you are angry with meant something different and there is no need to be so angry.

In general it appears that if you suffer from a traumatic experience or a tragedy instead of dealing with it only with frustration it may also help to try and find benefits from the situation as this really can help you recover faster.

In one study researchers interviewed a large sample of men who had a heart attack. They found that those who perceived benefits from their unfortunate episode recovered more quickly and reduced their risk from further heart attacks. The researchers found that eight years later, the group that began to appreciate life more, or looked at life in a more positive way, or didn't anger as much, had fewer recurrences than those who attributed their problems to others and maintained their frustration and anger.

For most minor situations, if you find that unearthing the benefits in anger provoking events difficult, here are some tried and tested techniques that can help to restore your equilibrium quickly.

(1) Take a few deep breaths from your diaphragm as this helps you to counter stress and relax a little

(2) Slowly repeat a neutral word such as 'one' over and over again. This simple form of meditation, focusing on a word for a couple of minutes can help to calm your anger

(3) If the opportunity presents itself take a walk for a few minutes

(4) Use visualization techniques to picture a relaxing setting, like a warm beach, or a pleasant holiday you have had

There are two more techniques worth mentioning. One is that from Cognitive Behavior Therapy (CBT) which requires you to challenge your assumptions and the other is from a Buddhist approach that requires patient acceptance.

Let us look at the CBT approach first:

In this approach, try to challenge your thinking. So instead of thinking, what a horrible person or what a so and so, he/she is you could say what he/she said wasn't very sensitive, may be I can confront this person later and say assertively how my feelings have been hurt. Alternatively, you could think, may be I over - reacted, perhaps I could apologize this time. Or again, you could think perhaps he/she meant something else and I have mis-understood, let me try to clarify the position. Basically, every time you are trying to challenge your angry thoughts by substituting more productive and less confrontational thoughts. With practice this approach becomes automatic and you can deal with your anger more assertively rather than aggressively.

Now let us look at patient acceptance approach. This method from the Buddhist tradition has become quite popular recently and is backed by scientific research to be helpful.

The basic premise of this methodology is that by practicing patience and accepting people's 'faults' non-judgmentally you become more tolerant and less angry. In fact this approach not only helps you to deal with anger but also has been shown to make you happier.

It is best practiced regularly even when you are not angry so that the response to anger can be more productive. Remember, once you are angry it is very difficult to control its consequences so practicing 'before the event' scenarios can really help.

For example, you can practice by visualizing some one insulting you. Then see if you can deal with the anger that arises by reasoning. You could say something like 'may be this person who insulted me was in a bad mood' or may be 'I wouldn't want to deal with him or her any way', so it's not worthwhile getting angry. Then try deep breathing for a minute or two.

Practicing this type of non-retaliatory patience will help you to behaviorally condition yourself to a more patient approach. And patience is an excellent anti-dote to anger. In principle this is similar to the modern CBT approach, except that in 'patient acceptance' you try to practice 'anger management' techniques as described above in advance of the event by simulating similar environments as often as possible, including being forgiving when possible.

Giving and Volunteering

Happiness comes when your work and words are of benefit to yourself and others.

Buddha

Chapter 11

Giving and Volunteering

We intuitively know that being kind and altruistic to others can be both purposeful in helping them as well as engendering a sense of fulfillment within ourselves.

In fact, most religions sensitize us or constantly remind us of the need to be charitable, philanthropic and kind. Charity is seen as a hallmark of faith. In Christianity, Islam, Hinduism, Buddhism and many other traditions the practice of charity is encouraged since it is seen to impart justice and act as a leveler to those in need. Tithing is encouraged in traditional Judaist and Christian religions. In Islam, it is mandatory to give Zakat, a portion of your wealth, to charity. Its purpose, as we have seen, is to balance out social inequality by assisting those most in need.

Interestingly, in Islam there is a second type of charity which is non-mandatory or voluntary called Sadaqah. This, for the believers is said to help them grow spiritually, to make them free from greed and malevolence so they can experience peace and happiness here and now as well as prepare them for the here after.

In Buddhism one is encouraged to reflect on poverty and misery in order to help us to become more conscious of deprivations and disadvantages in our societies and then follow it up by the practice of compassion by giving either time or money. This practice is said to help us achieve liberation from suffering and experience joy here and now.

Of course you don't have to have any of these beliefs or be religious to practice charity, but research has shown that those who have faith tend to give more than those who don't. Perhaps this is more to do with sensitization and training in giving then religion per se. As the Dalai Lama has reminded us, we need to practice compassion so that it becomes second nature. A few of us may be naturally compassionate but for the rest of us any reminders as those conferred by religion or moral philosophy may nudge us into acting. If there is constantly a collection box for charity in our local church it is difficult not to give.

We have seen that the belief of practicing charity is quite widespread and we know that it can confer tangible benefits to the receiving party or parties. What, however is the scientific evidence that it gives us happiness here and now?

Stephen Post a researcher has shown that volunteers who regularly help even in small ways, experience a 'givers' high. Interestingly, this feeling of well - being provides more health benefits than you would get if you exercised or stopped smoking. Imagine your health benefits if you engage in giving to charities or volunteering your time as well as exercising and not smoking

Elizabeth Dunn, another researcher, found that those who spend money on others feel happier than those who spend more on themselves.

The one neat thing about 'helping' or 'giving' is that it's a win –win. The recipient and the giver both benefit, albeit in different ways.

We can't all start a Bill Gates Foundation, or give away significant sums of money to charities, or volunteer huge amounts of time, but giving in ways however small confers greater happiness than not giving at all. Acts of giving or kindness could be simple things like listening to a friend more attentively, smiling to a colleague, giving a couple of dollars to a homeless person, sponsoring a child in Africa or, of course, volunteering a little of your time for good causes.

Here is some more research into the widespread benefits of giving and volunteering. Research done in the UK by Professor Paul Whitely found that not only did people feel happier and healthier but crime rates were reduced in areas which had implemented community based voluntary programs. In this study, 101 random districts in the UK were selected and relationships were mapped between the level of volunteerism and crime rate, as well as happiness levels. It turns out that those areas with a higher number of community based voluntary programs had happier communities, lower crime rates and even higher educational attainments. Correlation, of course, does not imply causation, but this study does provide a possible indication of the relationship between volunteering and reductions in crime rates.

Another study found that in older people those that engaged in volunteering activities had lower heart disease and lived longer than peers who didn't. Volunteering that involves interacting with people helps engender a social connectedness which has its own benefits. We know that social connectedness can give our mental health a boost.

Researchers have even quantified the amount of volunteering you need to do to experience these significant benefits. It appears that if we commit between 40 and 100 hours a year we will see corresponding happiness and health benefits.

Sonja Lyubminsky in her research on 'kindness' activities found that varying your activities periodically confers optimal benefits. It appears that we adapt to or get bored with doing the same thing. So if you regularly give money to the homeless you may want to occasionally give a bigger tip to a waiter, or you may want to give to other causes. What you give in terms of time or money will no doubt depend on your values, beliefs, priorities as well as your personal circumstances.

Below I will list some of my favorite charities. Naturally, I will be writing favorably about them and will no doubt show my bias. But, hopefully, these examples will be inspirational rather than a prescription of charities that you should subscribe to.

Kiva, which has its headquarters in San Francisco, is a web based micro finance organization. Kiva allows you to loan as little as $25 to poor individual entrepreneurs in developing parts of the world. These individuals are in turn associated with other legitimate micro finance organizations that partner with Kiva for funding. The neat thing about this charity is that, according to their statistics, more than 98% of the monies are returned back to the donor. This, of course, means that, upon repayment, you can recycle most of your money to another budding entrepreneur if you so wish. Alternatively, you can take your money out knowing that you have done some 'good' to some one with a real need. The concept of micro credit is that small amounts of loans, say $50 to $100, are often sufficient to give poor but enterprising individuals a start in life. Kiva, of course, got its inspiration from Professor Muhammed Yunus who started micro finance and established the Grameen bank. Grameen has lent hundreds of millions of dollars, in miniscule amounts, to poor but enterprising individuals in order to lift them out of poverty. Muhammed Yunus discovered that poor people when offered the chance for getting loans tend to repay them in their entirety with a high probability of success. They do this even when compared to normal credit worthy individuals in advanced economies. Muhammed Yunus eventually won the Nobel Prize for peace for his contribution to eradicating poverty.

Should micro finance inspire you then you can register at www.Kiva.org and donate as little as $25, to individual(s) you wish, in one of the many parts of the developing world. You will be updated regularly with progress reports as well as when appropriate repayments have been made.

Another one of my favorite charities is Focus Humanitarian, run by the Aga Khan Development Network. Focus Humanitarian works with leading international agencies in disaster relief across many countries. It plays a leading role in rescue and recovery operations including providing food and shelter during natural disasters. These include earthquakes, floods, hurricanes or where refugees result from war torn regions such as Afghanistan. You can find out more about them at:

www.focushumanitarian.com

My wife and I also have a weakness for Oxfam and Save the Children, both based in the UK. These charities are, of course, well known, operate across many countries and do some amazing work.

There are literally tens of thousands of Charities from mega operations like the Gates Foundation, founded by Bill & Melinda Gates to small ones such as your local community project. No doubt you will have your favorite causes and concerns. Whether you give to an established charity or you raise funds for a local community project, it is good to give. Amazingly, you will be doing your bit to help too. Giving as we have seen is a win-win.

We have mentioned some charities you can donate money to, but of course you can also give of your time and knowledge. It could simply be tutoring for free at your local college, or volunteering for a project that interests you through Voluntary Services Organization (VSO), or helping in the Citizen's Advice Bureau. Like charities, the list for voluntary organizations that you can give your time and knowledge to is endless.

Go with the Flow

It does not seem to be true that work necessarily needs to be unpleasant. It may always have to be hard, or at least harder than doing nothing at all. But there is ample evidence that work can be enjoyable, and that indeed, it is often the most enjoyable part of life

Mihaly Csikszentmihalyi

Chapter 12

Go with the Flow

Many of us have experienced occasions when time goes quickly specially when we are engaged in doing something we like and are enjoying ourselves. It could be at work when we are involved in a task that interests us, it could be when we are attending to our hobby or pet project, learning something new, or it could be when we are with someone we like being with.

Experiencing flow for me happens sometimes when I am reading a book that interests me or when I am writing or I am having a night out dinning with my spouse and our mutual friends. Likewise time goes quickly for me when I watch 'feel good' or inspiring movies and I feel engaged when I attend my Tai Chi class.

The term flow was coined by, Mihaly Csikszentmihalyi (pronounced Chick-sent-me-hi) Csikszentmihalyi's research into the creative process in the 1960's led him to observe that many artists, who were working on their painting, became so absorbed with their work that they ignored hunger, discomfort and even fatigue at that time. The concept of 'flow' came to his mind at this time.

Here are some interesting observations. Roughly one in five people experience 'flow' several times a day; on the other hand, about 15 percent claim they never experience it. For example, in a survey in Germany of approximately 6,500 people, when asked to rate their daily flow experiences, they responded as follows: 23 percent experienced flow often, 40 percent experienced it sometimes, with 25 percent experiencing flow rarely and 12 percent never experiencing it or not sure if they experienced it.

These statistical findings seem quite stable and universal.

However, rather than relying on the respondents memories on whether they experienced flow or not, Csikszentmihalyi developed a more precise method of studying flow.

He developed the Experience Sampling Method or ESM at the University of Chicago in the early 1970's.

This methodology has been applied to several studies and has collected data from approximately 2300 respondents. So what is its approach and finding?

This method allows one to collect data from a person's daily activity and experiences. This is done neatly through arranging a signal of a pager or watch to go off at random times within each two-hour segment of the day. When the signal goes off the respondent writes down in a booklet where they are, what they are doing, what they are thinking about, who they are with and finally to rate their experiences on various numerical scales. This study, which has also been done in countries other than the USA, found that flow occurs when an individual is involved in an absorbing task and usually when performing their favorite activity. This could be when they are cooking their favorite meal, listening to music, talking to friends, learning a new skill and, surprisingly quite frequently at work. On the other hand individuals rarely experienced flow when engaged in leisure activities like watching TV or even when just relaxing.

Now, you may be wondering, it's fine if you have an interesting job or have an engaging hobby. What about for the average person working 10 hours a day, 6 days a week and feeling totally exhausted at the end of the day?

Fortunately, there are many ways to increase flow in your life. We will look at a few approaches shortly. However, let's look at the work situation first. Let's assume that you have a boring job working as a supermarket cashier.

It appears that cashiers who pay more attention to their customers and engage in 'small talk' feel much more engaged, happier and less tired at the end of the day. The same, of course, applies to other jobs. A physician for example who listens carefully to his patients and who is genuinely interested in his patients will not only feel more engaged and happier but the patient too will have a more rewarding experience.

You may just be lucky and have a job that involves problem solving; for example, writing a computer program, solving a mathematical problem or doing some financial analysis in which case absorption and engagement in these or similar tasks might be much easier. But, as you can see what ever your job you can easily add to your enjoyment by tweaking it a little and finding more meaning in it.

Now let us look at two more approaches to increasing your flow:

Increasing flow through attention

Attention to every day events can help us engage more with the present. Attention to every day tasks can not only helps us to feel more involved but more often to experience joy as well. Consider the generally pleasurable activity of conversation. Sometimes when conversing with someone, for example a friend, we tend to pre-judge, knowing what's coming next and often interrupt with our views and opinions. Next time, when in conversation with a friend or even an acquaintance try to listen more attentively, without pre- judgment or interruptions. Although this is quite hard to do with practice you can learn the art of 'attentiveness'. You might pleasantly surprise yourself that by listening more carefully and fully you will gain a new perspective, may be understand a little more than you might otherwise and without doubt your friend will feel much more rewarded and comforted. Sometimes we can try this technique even with our partner! We all like to be listened to without interruptions. But the paradox is that by listening more attentively and more compassionately you will gradually feel much more engaged and involved, rather than being bored and of course your friend or partner will feel more listened to. In other words you may find the act of listening itself much more satisfying and enjoyable and the temptation to interrupt will be less resulting in a win-win situation.

We can, of course, apply the principle of attentiveness to any task or activity. Consider washing dishes which most people consider boring and are probably just waiting to finish this activity so that they can go on to do the next task. However, by attending to your washing up process, noticing the flow of water, or the saucepans becoming cleaner you make your task more enjoyable and engaging. Your perception of 'time' going slowly will change to 'time' going much more quickly.

Attentiveness is often taught in Buddhism as a form of meditative exercise, but you do not have to subscribe to any beliefs to benefit from being more focused or more attentive to every day tasks. Paradoxically, this act of disciplining the mind helps us feel less stressful and more joyful.

Pick activities that you enjoy

Although we have seen that 'attentiveness' can make even the most mundane job more bearable, or even enjoyable, it obviously helps if you can choose an activity that you find interesting in the first place.

Listening to your favorite music, going dancing, swimming, playing golf, or going for a long walk can all help you to experience positive emotions and increase your flow. Try and choose one or two activities regularly that you enjoy or think you could enjoy and see the difference it makes to your life. Maybe it could be going to see a particular type of movie once week, reading an inspiring novel or going to the opera another week and going out for a social the third week.

As adults we are often pre-occupied with our work and daily affairs and sometimes forget to 'enjoy' or 'get involved' with the things we like.

Gaining flow for a more sustained duration requires engagement in a task that you can get really involved in. For example, learning a new skill or undertaking a new project that you always wanted to do. The critical requirement for flow is to set a goal that's challenging but not impossible to achieve. Undertake a project that you will find interesting and one that is matched by your ability. If it is too difficult, you may feel too stressed. Conversely if it is too easy you may get easily bored. Accept that in any project there will be set - backs.

Starting a new project can be a challenge in itself. If you find yourself procrastinating, remember research shows that the hardest part of starting a new project is the beginning. When you start your project break it down into manageable chunks so that you can start doing at least the first bit. Make sure this first chunk isn't too long. Preferably it should be short in terms of time, maybe just a few minutes to start with. When you finish this first bit you will feel more in control of your accomplishment to date and this should provide you with further motivation to keep you going.

Increasing your positive experiences regularly by experiencing flow in ways that require engagement or attention can also help you to build up your 'reservoir' of happiness so that you have more to draw from in difficult times.

Forgiving

Forgiveness is the fragrance the violet sheds on the heel that has crushed it

Mark Twain

Chapter 13

Forgiving

We intuitively know that holding grudges can be emotionally stressful for us. Several studies have confirmed this. Dr Fred Luskin, Director of Stanford Forgiveness Project and author of "Forgive for Good' confirms that holding grudges, being resentful and being bitter can be damaging both for your emotional health as well as your Cardio Vascular Health.

The corollary, of course is that forgiveness can act as an antidote and be beneficial for our health. For example, in one study it was found that practicing forgiveness improves your immune system from colds and flu's.

In another study involving 260 volunteers, Fred Luskin observed many benefits in participants who learn to forgive. These volunteers were given nine hours of training in forgiveness. Various psychological measurements took place, both before and after this study. The outcomes were impressive. This exercise in forgiveness helped participants to lower their stress levels, boost their self- confidence as well as engender a greater sense of social connectedness. In addition, they reported fewer headaches, backaches and upset stomachs than they previously had.

Another study with AIDS patients found that when these patients forgave those individuals who had infected them in the first place, they were able to cope better with their illness and suffer from less malaise.

In addition, a study conducted at the University of Michigan Institute of Social Research found that forgiveness is associated with better physical and mental health.

Unfortunately, forgiving even small transgressions may not be easy for some people. For major emotional hurts or abuse it is of course very difficult to forgive. Forgiveness in this case should not be confused with accepting this behavior in the first place. It is more a question of having fewer grudges and less bitterness about an event that has long passed.

Sometimes of course we ourselves may have hurt someone, either unwittingly or through some thoughtlessness.

How can we then learn to forgive appropriately?

Sonja Lyubormisky in her book 'The How of Happiness,' recommends writing a forgiveness letter as one of the strategies. In this letter, which you don't have to send, you can express how hurt you were, how it affected you and that you found this behavior unacceptable. However, you do not want to harbor bitterness and grudges forever, so you will forgive this person for say 'humiliating you in front of your friends' or whatever the reason may be.

If you still feel the hurt after many years have passed and additionally feel that you can never forgive this person, and that one day you will make this individual pay or you want this person to be hurt and be miserable, then it appears you may benefit even more from the practice of forgiveness.

If you wish to explore the idea further, you may find more strategies suggested by Dr Luskin in his book 'Forgive for Good'.

You can also practice forgiveness for smaller transgressions by yourself and others by simply practicing Loving Kindness Meditation as explained earlier.

It is worth remembering, that religious schools of thinking are very clear on the benefit of forgiveness. Consider the examples below from Christianity and Islam respectively.

Then Peter came to Jesus and asked, "Lord, how many times shall I forgive my brother when he sins against me? Up to seven times?" Jesus answered, "I tell you not seven times, but seventy-seven times.

Mathew 18:21-22

And verily, whosoever shows patience and forgiveness, that would, truly be from things recommended by Allah. (42:43)

Exercise

Walking is the best possible exercise. Habituate yourself to walk very far

Thomas Jefferson

Chapter 14

Exercise

We all know that exercise can help us to remain fit, reduce weight, increase happiness and even prevent heart disease. In fact a significant amount of research backs up these assertions. Consider heart disease. It appears no matter how careful you are with your diet you are at higher risk from heart disease if you don't exercise. Exercise, it seems, is an independent variable for reducing the risk from coronary heart disease (CHD).

Being physically fit halves your risk from CHD because it:

(1) Reduces blood pressure

(2) Increases HDL (the 'good' cholesterol)

(3) Decreases LDL (the 'bad' cholesterol)

(4) Helps weight loss

(5) Helps your heart function more efficiently

Researchers at Duke University suggest it is the amount of exercise rather than the intensity that has the maximum impact on improving blood cholesterol levels. They also found that any exercise is better than no exercise although more is generally better. We will discuss optimal exercise levels later but first, we will explore a few more benefits of exercise.

Most of us also know that exercise can help reduce stress and lift our moods. Recent research shows that exercise can in fact combat clinical depression, protect us from brain disease and even help us to reduce cravings. Consider the research on depression

In a report produced by Lynette L. Craft and Frank M Perna in 2004 on the benefits of exercise for the clinically depressed the following findings emerged:

They analyzed studies on various exercise regimes. They found that just 30 minutes of treadmill walking for 10 consecutive days was sufficient to produce a significant reduction in depression compared to control groups who undertook no exercise.

In another study where a group exercised for 12 consecutive weeks, their long- term well being in terms of reduced depressive symptoms lasted for at least 12 months.

Here is another interesting finding. Exercise regimes were compared to Cognitive Behavior Therapy (CBT) and a combination of running and CBT. There was no significant difference between these 3 groups; in other words, all 3 groups exhibited a significant reduction in their depressive symptoms.

In another study by Blumenthal et al, exercise regimes were compared to psychotropic drugs. 3 groups were followed. Those in the exercise group walked or jogged at 70% to 85% of their suggested heart rate for 30 minutes, 3 times a week for 16 weeks. The second group just took the medication and the third group took a combination of exercise and medication. After 16 weeks, there was no significant difference in the treatment groups in terms of the benefits gained although the group receiving drugs improved their depressive symptoms much more quickly. Further, a 10 month follow up showed that participants in the exercise group had lower rates of depression than those on medication.

Many reasons have been proposed as to why exercise lifts mood.

One of the reasons is the endorphin hypothesis, which asserts that these feel good hormones which are released when you exercise, make you feel happier and thus reduce your depressive symptoms.

One other possibility is the distraction hypothesis. This asserts that whilst exercising you give yourself some breathing space from negative thinking and ruminations. Exercise acts as a type of meditation that helps you to focus on the here and now rather than on negative thinking. The cumulative effect of these temporary respites gradually builds your positive experiences and thus reduces your negativity.

In reality it is probably both these factors, not forgetting the cardio vascular benefits that accrue from the aerobic activity.

Exercise is good for your brain

Several studies done by Gomez-Pinilla and his team at the University of California show that exercise actually helps the regeneration of damaged cells. These studies seem to indicate that exercise may protect against Parkinson's disease and even reverse some of the devastating consequences of traumatic brain injury.

A further study by Richard Smeyne and his colleagues at Saint Jude Children's Research Hospital in Memphis in a lab model mimicking human tissue seems to indicate that exercise may help slow the progression of Parkinson's disease or, if started early in life may prevent the disease from ever developing.

An international team of researchers has also found that the feel good chemical beta-endorphins released during exercise may be the key factor for this beneficial effect. It seems that beta-endorphins released during exercise help in the production of new neurons, in the hippocampus, a brain region involved in learning and memory.

Dr John Ratey at the Harvard Medical School has observed that vigorous exercise leads to smarter brains; for example kids' scores in math and science improve. He also found that individuals with ADD/ADHD could improve their focus and attention span significantly.

Finally, his investigations also confirmed that even small amounts of regular exercise could help most of us to ward off memory decline.

This latter finding is good news for all of us as exercise also helps to keep our minds alert and potentially delay the onset of memory loss during old age.

Exercise can reduce our cravings

Research at the University of Exeter in the UK has suggested that exercise can reduce nicotine cravings. A number of studies back this up and show that smokers report reduced cravings after exercising.

It appears that for smokers who want to give up this habit, exercise seems a viable alternative to pharmaceutical products such as nicotine patches. Even fifteen minutes of walking, jogging or cycling can help a smoker to kick this habit. Exercise for 15 minutes before you feel like smoking. This it seems is sufficient to refrain for a few hours. Keep repeating this until you no longer smoke and then revert to doing 15 minutes, every day and then gradually you can reduce it to just 3 times a week. (Note, initially you may have to exercise for 15 minutes, three or four times a day for this strategy to be effective.)

How much exercise do you need for all the different benefits?

The exercise regime for giving up smoking has already been outlined. We will now consider the requirement in its duration and intensity for our general well – being.

A 30 minute brisk walk three times a week is sufficient to improve your fitness level, reduce your cardio-vascular risk, improve your mood as well as keep you mentally alert right into old age.

Of course, if you can exercise for 5 days out of seven this is even better. But there is no need to be punitive as additional exercise in terms of duration, beyond a certain level doesn't seem to confer any more benefits.

You could, however, increase the intensity as you get fitter, although this too is not strictly necessary unless you want to be super fit and gain additional benefits of a much sharper memory. Another way to measure your exercise level is to keep track of the number of steps you take daily. For this, you may want to invest in a pedometer which records this activity. Experts recommend accumulating 10,000 steps every day.

Remember all activities count. Walking to the shops, doing household chores, doing gardening or climbing stairs. You can try parking your car further than you normally do when going shopping or going to work.

When jogging or walking briskly remember not to exert yourself. The advice is to start at 65% of your maximum age related heart rate and gradually increase this to around 80%. The formula for working this out is to subtract your age from 220 and multiply it by the appropriate percentage. So for example for some one aged, 40 the maximum heart rate you should aim for is 65% of, 180. This works out to 117 beats per minute. Gradually you can increase your maximum heart- rate to 80% of 180, which works out to be 144.

We have seen that exercise has many benefits, not forgetting its significant impact on increasing happiness too.

Anxiety, Social Anxiety & Depression – CBT May Help You

People and things do not upset us rather we upset ourselves by believing that they can upset us

Albert Ellis

Chapter 15

Anxiety, Social Anxiety & Depression – CBT May Help You

So far we have looked at happiness building strategies that can help us improve our mood and increase our well-being. It is worth looking at Cognitive Behavior Therapy (CBT) as an additional tool that can help us remove our mental distress in the first place. CBT was pioneered by Aaron Beck and is now generally a well-established method for treating depression, anxiety and phobias. Thanks to extensive clinical trials as robust as those in pharmacology for medical interventions, CBT has been found to have a high success rate.

It is effective against panic disorder, obsessive-compulsive disorder, depression and even post-traumatic stress.

Any sufferer from these problems will find it difficult to believe that CBT can help. Take depression for example; when a low mood strikes someone it is not easy to pick oneself up. Even worse is to suggest 'just start CBT and you will be fine'.

The anguish and despair one feels when in a depressed mood can be overwhelming. Even when you are in a better frame of mind you may be pre-occupied with when the next downward cycle will occur. This empty feeling coupled with uncertainty makes every day living onerous.

Similarly, someone who has suffered emotional trauma may think that their problem is far too complex to be solved with CBT. May be they should consult a psycho-analyst who can probe into the depths of their psyche. Fortunately, this is not necessary and may even be counter-productive. As mentioned earlier CBT can help depression, emotional traumas, obsessive-compulsive disorders and phobias with a high degree of success. In fact, the benefits of CBT have been shown to be more durable with lower relapse rates than drugs.

In addition, other therapies which are also based on cognitive psychology, such as family therapy and behavioral couples-based therapy, have been shown to be helpful for other problems. For example, behavioral couples therapy has been helpful for alcoholics to stay sober.

So how does CBT actually work?

The basic premise of CBT is that our thoughts, or type of thinking, determine our behaviors and feelings. In a person with depression the thinking may go something like this: ' I'm no good', 'I'm a loser' and 'my future is hopeless'. The individual who is depressed automatically thinks like this when faced with the smallest challenge or set back. Even in the absence of any setbacks he or she may ruminate about being useless or being a failure. Unfortunately, these negative thoughts in turn lead to feeling low and a depressive mood which then goes on to perpetuate this type of thinking. We saw earlier that troublesome thoughts tend to repeat themselves and are difficult to suppress.

How can this cycle of negative thinking and depression be stopped?

The first step is for the individual (usually with the help of a therapist) to recognize this feedback loop in which distorted thoughts cause the negative feelings. The basic method is then to challenge and gradually replace these negative thoughts with more realistic thinking. E.g. 'I'm a loser' – with 'I'm not always a loser' Try and find instances however small where you have succeeded. Or in the case where the individual ruminates 'my future is hopeless' you can challenge this with 'my future may or may not be hopeless' or 'in all probability I will have some good outcomes and some bad outcomes'. It is important to be realistic as you are more likely to accept this type of 'new' thinking so that it helps you to remove this cycle of despair.

Try and avoid unrealistic substitutions as suggested by some self-help gurus. For example 'from now on I will feel better and better and all my troubles will go away' as this approach may make the situation worse.

Ideally, you need to work with a CBT professional to help you recognize your own negative feedback loops and work out a plan of action which is beneficial to you. Usually you should see some improvement after eight to twelve sessions.

Gradually you will learn to replace your negative and distorted thinking with more productive and realistic thinking which in turn will have a beneficial effect on your mood. The CBT therapist will usually suggest other 'common sense' ways to lift your mood.

You will learn that instead of 'ruminating' it is better to engage in some distraction activities like going for a walk, or going to buy a newspaper or simply smiling for 30 seconds! In fact we saw earlier the powerful effect that smiling and laughter can have on our mood for a very long time.

If your depression is very severe or you are having suicidal thoughts you first need to consult your physician for some anti-depressants and then benefit from these CBT techniques later. The benefits of changes due to CBT training will ultimately lead to permanent behavioral changes. CBT has also been successfully applied in Phobias and Social Anxiety, where the client is gradually exposed to the feared situation and made to realize that overwhelming fear or shame can gradually recede. CBT is not a cure all but you have a significantly higher chance of improving than just a placebo effect. Clinical trials have consistently demonstrated high success rates for CBT.

CBT can be useful for 'curing' ordinary shortfalls as well. For example you may be afraid of giving presentations, or articulating your view- point with confidence, or you may find it hard to say 'no'. I say 'ordinary', because other than those particular situations these individuals seem to function well. So how do you tackle 'ordinary' shortfalls?

The main principles in making CBT work for you are as follows:

(1) Assess your present beliefs about your concern or shortfall

(2) Assess the evidence that this is necessarily true

(3) Try to finding alternative explanations

(4) Create a plan of action to experiment with new ideas

(5) Collect data from new action & revise views

(6) Rebuild confidence with changed behavior

Let us look at a specific example: **'Fear of making a fool of myself in a social situation'**

Accompanying Feelings: Self- criticism, shame, self doubt and feeling very uncomfortable

Present belief: I don't like to be in a social group as people might think I am strange; also I might make a fool of myself

Evidence: There are, many times where I feel extremely uncomfortable in a group. I don't know what people think, they probably think I am stupid and I never seem to have anything to say

Alternative explanation 1: It seems there are instances when I feel ok and can say quite a lot

Alternative explanation 2: Some people may be very glad to have me in their company

Alternative explanation 3: I notice that most people just indulge in small talk and seem to be pre-occupied with them selves

Alternative explanation 4: Perhaps they don't think that I am strange

Alternative explanation 5: I have never actually noticed making a fool of myself, and even if I did they may not think anything of it

Plan of action: I will test some of these assumptions in the following way

(1) I will see what others typically talk about

(2) I will test their reaction when I engage in small talk

(3) I will see if I can socialize with individuals first

(4) I will try socializing with individuals more frequently

(5) I will try socializing with groups when the opportunity arises

Collect Data & Revise Views

(6) I will continue to revise this process until it works

(7) May be I could ask one of my friends for his or her opinion

(8) Evidence so far seems to be mixed, sometimes my socialization goes well, sometimes I still feel anxious

(9) It appears that my belief that I appear strange may have been misguided

(10) I need to work on this until my confidence improves much more

Obviously, each case will be different, and for some the process will take longer than others, but you can see that the guiding principle is to challenge your assumptions, argue with yourself and experiment with new approaches. It seems that as your thinking is challenged gradually your feelings and behavior change.

When feelings of self-criticism, shame and self-doubt overwhelm us it seems impossible to conceive that we can ever change our thinking. Further, our rationalizing mind convinces us that probably CBT can work for others but not for us, as our problem is somehow much deeper than any one else's.

When this type of negative self-talk occurs, rest assured that it is common to think in this way. One way out of this dilemma is to keep challenging your assumptions. You will be pleasantly surprised how your behavior changes towards your desired goal in a relatively short time.

In addition we can supplement CBT with several happiness techniques that we learnt earlier since these can help us increase our feelings from normality to even greater happiness.

Reduce Your Risk of Heart Disease & Strokes by Increasing Your Social Connectedness and Controlling Your Anger

Friendship makes prosperity more shining and lessens adversity by dividing and sharing it

Cicero

Chapter 16

Reduce Your Risk of Heart Disease and Strokes by Increasing your Social Connectedness and Controlling your Anger

Consider Coronary Heart Disease (CHD), which has reached chronic proportions in the developed world. We have already seen that anger, hostility and rage can adversely affect the risk of CHD.

We will see that social connectedness too is just as important as high-risk conventional factors such as cholesterol, high blood pressure, smoking and lack of exercise in reducing the incidence of heart disease. Initially, let us explore the so-called conventional factors as these are equally important. Amongst health conscious individuals it is now fashionable to talk about one's cholesterol level. What is less well known is that a low cholesterol level does not necessarily mean there is low risk of CHD. Conversely, a high cholesterol level does not necessarily mean there is a high risk. We will see an example below shortly to illustrate this point. However, the more health conscious individual will already know that factors such as HDL and LDL are important when calculating your overall cholesterol risk. HDL or high-density lipoproteins can be thought of as the 'good' cholesterol.

Conversely, LDL or low-density lipoproteins can be thought of as the 'bad' cholesterol. It turns out that a high HDL gives some protection whereas a high LDL increases your risk even further. Also, the ratio of your total cholesterol to your HDL, as well as knowing your LDL level, gives you a much better risk assessment.

Consider the example of two males of similar height and weight and lifestyle habits with the following values of total cholesterol and HDL levels. (We will consider other factors later)

This information is represented in table form in the next page with individuals A & B.

	A	B
Total Cholesterol (mg/dl)	200	240
HDL	40	60
Ratio: (Total Cholesterol/ HDL)	5	4

You will notice that based just on the total cholesterol values B has a higher risk from CHD than A. On the other hand, based on just the HDL values, A seems to be at greater risk. Also, based on the ratio of total cholesterol to the HDL value it turns out that it is in fact A that has a higher probability of CHD. It is worth noticing that if A also had an elevated LDL reading then A's risk would be significantly higher than B rather than just a little higher than B

The reader probably knows that to accurately compute the risk of heart disease you need to consider many other factors.

There are many free risk assessment calculators on the net that do the work for you. For instance the website at the American Heart Association or the Mayo clinic will give you quite a comprehensive analysis and work out your 10 year risk from getting a heart attack. Armed with this information the health conscious individual will know more about CHD risk factors than the average general practitioner.

Social Connectedness

Here is something interesting - studies done on individuals who have a high level of social connectedness show a significantly reduced risk of CHD (up to 50% less) than those that don't, assuming all other risk factors stay the same.

This means having friends, family connections and belonging to groups can be as helpful for your well being as well as reducing your overall risk of CHD as tackling conventional risk factors like cholesterol levels.

In fact, Robert Putnam from Harvard University and the author of Bowling Alone observed that, "if you belong to no groups but decide to join one, you cut your risk of dying over the next year by half". This is interesting because it means you cut your risk from CHD, strokes, and any other illness by half by belonging to a group.

Here are some specific studies that illustrate this more clearly.

A study done by Sheldon Cohen et al from Carnegie Mellon University found that belonging to groups or having a social network made people less susceptible to the common cold. Their work, which was published in Psychological Science, established that the least sociable group in their study were twice as likely to get colds as those who were the most sociable although the more sociable group were probably exposed to many more germs.

In more recent study, published in 2008 in Neuropsychological Rehabilitation, Haslam, Haslam, Jetten together with other psychologists at the University of Exeter in England, examined the changing circumstances of 53 people who had recently suffered from a stroke. They observed that life satisfaction after the stroke was much higher for those who belonged to social groups before their stroke. Analysis showed that the support from their respective groups was a critical factor in their quality of life and resilience after their stroke.

It turns out that participation in group life, be it belonging to a bridge club, a yoga group, a dancing group, a reading club or whatever, is akin to having a vaccination giving you additional resilience and health protection without any nasty side effects. It is also the case that belonging to multiple groups is probably the optimal strategy for building the highest level of resilience as well as protecting yourself from CHD.

Anger

As we have seen, anger, hostility and rage can be equally detrimental to your health and can also increase your risk of heart disease by more than 50%. If you have difficulty in controlling your anger the chapter on anger management may help you.

Similarly, those who anger less easily are also less prone to heart disease than those who frequently experience rage.

Anger, hostility and rage have also been shown to adversely affect your blood pressure and significantly increase the likelihood of a heart attack.

For the curious here are the main factors that affect your risk.

Major Risk factors that cannot be changed:

Age: Your risk increases as you age

Gender: Your risk is higher if you are male

Heredity (including race): If you have a history of heart disease in the family you have a higher risk. Likewise, if you are African American, Mexican American or Asian American or a South Asian in the UK you may be at higher risk.

Major Risk Factors that can be controlled:

Social Connectedness: Friends, family and group memberships can significantly lower your risk by up to 50%

Anger, hostility and rage: Controlling these can be as helpful as controlling your cholesterol levels and could well be beneficial for your blood pressure.

Smoking: Your risk starts to reduce significantly a few years after you give up

Diet: Try and eat less saturated fat & more fruit and vegetables

Blood Pressure: Should ideally be below 120/80 (The first value refers to the systolic and the second to the diastolic)

Cholesterol: Ideally your value should be below 200mg/dl

HDL: This is the 'good' cholesterol and should be higher than 45mg/dl

LDL: This is the bad cholesterol which should be less than 130mg/dl

Triglycerides: This is a type of fat which should be less 150mg/dl

Physical inactivity: If you are sedentary this is a significant risk factor

Obesity & overweight: Your weight should be in a range that is ideal for your height. In other words your body mass index should be in an ideal range.

Diabetes Mellitus: Unfortunately, diabetes significantly increases the risk of CHD

Here is a list of cholesterol values and what they mean:

Total Cholesterol Values:

160 –199 mg/dl   desirable

200 – 239 mg/dl   borderline High
240 – 279 mg/dl   high
280 mg/dl   very high

LDL Values:

Less than 100 mg/dl   optimal
100 – 129 mg/dl   near optimal
130 – 159 mg/dl   borderline high
160 – 189 mg/dl   high
190 + mg/dl   very high

HDL Values:

60 + mg/dl   optimal
50 – 59 mg/dl   near optimal
45 – 49 mg/dl   good
40 – 44 mg/dl   average risk
35 – 39 mg/dl   moderate risk
less than 35 mg/dl   high risk

Blood Pressure:

The top number is your **systolic** blood pressure. (The highest pressure when your heart beats and pushes the blood round your body)

The bottom number is your **diastolic** blood pressure (The lowest pressure when your heart relaxes between beats)

Normal blood pressure: More than 90 over 60 (90/60) and less than 120 over 80 (120/80)

Nearly normal but not optimal: More than 120 over 80 and less than 140 over 90 (120/80-140/90)

High blood pressure possible: 140 over 90 (140/90) or higher (over a number of weeks)

High blood pressure possible: if your top number is 140 or more (regardless of what your bottom number is)

High blood pressure possible: if your bottom number is 90 or more (regardless what your top number is)

Low blood pressure possible: if your top number is 90 or less regardless of what your bottom number is.

Low blood pressure possible: if your bottom number is 60 or less regardless of what your top number is.

Triglycerides:

Less than 190 mg/dl is fine, but optimally it should be less than 150mg/dl

Ratio of Total cholesterol to HDL

Remember it's the ratio of your **Total Cholesterol** to your **HDL level** that is very important.

Anything less than 5 is healthy, but a ratio of 4.5 or less is optimal

Understanding the Psychology of Money and Managing Debt

Annual income twenty pounds, annual expenditure nineteen and six (pence), result, happiness. Annual income twenty pounds, annual expenditure twenty pound ought and six (pence), result misery.

Charles Dickens

Chapter 17

Understanding the Psychology of Money and Managing Debt

Many studies have shown that having more than a certain amount of money doesn't substantially add to your happiness. Once basic needs are met and you have accounted for food, shelter, basic security, allowance for entertainment, some holidays, then any additional monies you have tend to confer marginal returns in well-being. Richard Easterlin an economist at the University of Southern California compared the average levels of happiness of the US economy over the last fifty years with increasing gross national (GNP) product. He found that despite the fact that GNP has multiplied at least five fold in this time period happiness levels have remained flat. This is sometimes called the 'Easterlin paradox'.

In addition, studies have repeatedly shown that surplus money that is spent on others or charitable activities gives you far greater happiness than splashing out on a big-ticket item for yourself. If you do have surplus funds and you do not want to spend a significant amount on others, it is better to buy lots of small pleasurable experiences for yourself and your family or friends rather than a one big-ticket item. There are always exceptions, but generally this seems to hold true. We have seen before that a one off big-item purchase may lead to an initial boost in happiness, but we quickly revert to our baseline levels.

However, some of us struggle with keeping our budgets in balance and may even fear being perpetually in debt. Quite often this is because, unthinking we over spend, rather than because of lack of funds in the first place. Further, being in debt increases our anxiety and so reduces our well-being and happiness.

Many individuals find themselves in this situation and in debt. The glib answer to solving this problem is simply to take control of your spending habits. Habits as we know are extremely difficult to change. We always tend to rationalize our expenditures. Standard debt counseling advice is to make a note of your income, write down your expenses and try to balance your incomes with your expenditure.

Here, we will take a slightly different approach to controlling debt. Firstly, we will use a slightly more refined model for categorizing expenditure items as compared to standard advice and secondly we will try to understand that additional purchases beyond a certain amount, rarely lead to more happiness. We will finally try to crunch some actual numbers for additional insight.

To create a new habit you have to start somewhere.

(1) First understand that however clever or competent you may be if 'being in debt' is a problem then it is more than likely that you are overlooking many unnecessary purchases

(2) To facilitate this habit make a note of your expenses in the four categories mentioned below

(3) Finally, put into practice this activity for at least one month

Break down your expenses into four or five key categories:

You will see that if you or someone you know has expenses under category (5) professional psychological or medical help may be required.

(1) Critical Expenses:

These include food items, accommodation, house tax/service charges, utility, cell phones, internet- subscription, miscellaneous housing items such as soap, toothpaste, etc and transport costs

(2) Necessary Expenses:

These include car and life insurances,

(3) Quality of life items

These include basic entertainment costs, the odd bottle of wine, going out for a meal, basic holiday allowance, future-saving plans, some additional clothing and other personal items

(4) Unnecessary items

These include, buying unnecessary impulse purchases, big- ticket items that are not really necessary, additional entertainment, buying unnecessary gadgets

(5) Health ruining items:

These include cigarettes, excess alcohol, gambling and drugs

Let us assume that for the majority of our readers who find that they have debt problem, it is only the first four categories that we need to consider.

Clearly, every one needs items in category (1). Most people in advanced economies can enjoy items under (2) & (3). However, items in category (4) rarely add to your well - being. In fact it can be argued that regular consumption of items in this fourth category can lead to immense dissatisfaction. Research has consistently shown that one's happiness does not increase with increased spending beyond the basic necessities outlined under (1), (2) & (3).

Let's take a hypothetical income & expenditure account for a professional bachelor in his mid thirties living in the USA

Net monthly income:	**$3,500**
Critical Expenses:	
Expenses for Rent/Mortgage	$1200
Food & household items	$600
Miscellaneous	$100
Utilities	$90
House tax	$120
Telephone/internet	$70
Transport costs	$120
Sub-Total	**$2,300**

(2)

Necessary Expenses

Car insurance	$100
Car maintenance costs	$70
Accident & Travel Insurance	$10
Basic Life Insurance	$30
Credit card repayment	$220
Miscellaneous	$170

Sub-total	**$600**

(3) **Quality of life items**

Entertainment & outings	$100
Clothing allowance	$50
Holiday allowance	$150
Savings	$150
Miscellaneous	$100
Sub-total	**$550**

(4) **Unnecessary items**

More purchases	$150
More entertainment	$100
More gadgets	$100
More Miscellaneous	$150
Sub-total	**$500**

Grand Total Monthly Expenditure = $2,300 + $600 + $500 + $500 = $3900

Obviously, this is hypothetical example. The amounts that you will actually spend on these typical items will naturally differ as will your net income.

The crucial point is that by analyzing your expenses in categories, it will give you a quick idea at how much you are spending into each designated area.

A significant amount, almost two thirds of this hypothetical expenditure, goes into food and shelter. In fact this is not untypical. Finally, an equal amount is spent on necessary items (category 2) as is on quality of life items (category 3).

In this hypothetical example, this single professional seems to be in debt by $400 per month. This can of course accumulate to significant amounts over time. In this case some cutting down in the unnecessary category is essential. This will obviously vary significantly, but essentially it is this list that you need to worry about.

So how do you manage debt or advise someone to manage debt?

Clearly one needs to have a reasonable idea on how you are spending your money and what category it falls in. The initial mistake is to put many unnecessary items into the 'quality of life' list of items. You need to be more honest about this. If you find that all your items are in the third category then in the first month or two you need to start differentiating between these categories.

Gradually, your discrimination will improve. You will understand that the unnecessary extras, as itemized in category 4, do not add to your happiness. Once you can discriminate between 'necessary' and 'unnecessary' items you will not only be much happier but you will have your finances in better shape too.

After Thoughts and Concluding Remarks

Action may not always bring happiness, but there is no happiness without action

Benjamin Disraeli

Chapter 18

After Thoughts and Concluding Remarks

We have seen that gratitude, compassion, voluntary service, giving, praying for the benefit of others, social engagement, altruism, involvement in meaningful tasks and forgiveness are all acts that can lead to much more happiness and contentment. We have also seen that smiling, laughter, having fun, listening to music can also add to our pleasure and indeed to our reservoir of happiness. We have also seen that going for constant acquisition or the pursuance of hedonistic pleasure may give us a temporary lift in happiness but we soon return to our baseline level.

Additionally, we have explored how CBT can help us remove aspects of mental distress such as depression, phobias and emotional traumas.

However, improving our happiness and contentment seems to be more akin to following the virtues tradition. The approach to lasting happiness and peace is not new to those who believe in the 'middle' way as preached by all the major religions. For example "Love thy neighbor as thyself' and 'There can be no compulsion in religion" (2:256), or 'it is more blessed to give than to receive' are different dictates taken from just two religions. The former two from Christianity and the latter from Islam each clearly preach compassion, tolerance, acceptance and pluralism in their respective ways.

Although we constantly hear about the fundamental and radical versions of Islam, Christianity, Hinduism and Buddhism, fortunately they represent a small minority rather than the vast majority of 'moderate' and 'rationalist' followers. It does not seem inconsistent to have faith, be spiritual and also be a rational thinker. It appears that having faith and having meaning is another way to find contentment and peace.

On the other hand, fundamentalism of any type leads to intolerance, inflexibility and rigidity. Further it can also lead people to have a detrimental view about themselves as well as their communities. For example, research has shown that individuals who believe in original sin or those that attribute some health problems, as a punishment from God may feel reluctant to take medical treatment, often suffer from low self-esteem and suffer from more depression. In addition, radical views, as we have recently seen can have even a more deleterious effect on communities and societies. For example, by denying evolution, societies can potentially hinder scientific progress or by killing those who are of a different faith as in the case of some Taliban groups, they can terrorize, maim and kill innocent victims. Inflexible views can lead to more prejudice that denies the richness of diversity and pluralism.

The corollary to this, as I mentioned before and backed by significant research, is that those who have faith and practice the 'middle way' are happier than those that don't have faith. Faith of conviction leads to more happiness than faith of convenience.

Perhaps, the best course for those without faith is to look for meaning and arrive at a philosophical view that you are happy with. Many in this category look for beauty, grandeur and awe in nature and the people around them. This of course can be a life long process for some. Religion it seems provides us with ready - made answers to our needs that require searching for meaning as well as providing us with additional coping skills in time of significant stress. For many of us it also provides spiritual fulfillment and a sense of purpose.

Concluding remarks

On the next page, I have divided the happiness activities outlined in this book into 3 main categories. Hopefully, this summary will make it easier for you to choose the appropriate activities, depending on your interests and requirements. For example, choosing to incorporate some of the techniques in Category I will not take more of your time, it will just require small changes in your approach and the commitment to apply these techniques into your daily activities.

Some of the activities and techniques in Category II will take more time, but once you build a few of these into your daily routine you will experience higher levels of well being. If you choose nothing else try keeping a gratitude diary or journal as this has been shown to have a significant impact on happiness levels.

Activities in category III will give you the opportunity to experience more 'flow' and acquire additional coping skills for stressful times. In addition, by choosing to practice loving kindness meditation or mindfulness meditation you will experience long - term contentment and gain a sense of inner peace.

It is very likely that you already incorporate some of these activities in the three categories, outlined above, in your daily routine anyway. But you can add considerably to your repertoire and thus 'build and broaden' your happiness base even more. Try and pick at least two additional techniques or activities from each category and incorporate these into your every day life. You will find that in a short time you will experience more joy, enthusiasm and energy and be able to cope better in times of crisis.

Category I

Examples:

Have more fun

Be silly make faces in the mirror if necessary

Smile and laugh more (Even for 30 seconds per day)

Be more appreciative

Be more glad and thankful for the things you have

Walk more joyfully and vigorously, even for one minute, when walking somewhere

Category II

Be more grateful – undertake to write a gratefulness journal (If you decide to do nothing else – do this)

Read an inspiring novel

Watch a feel good movie

Listen to music that you enjoy

Go out for a meal with a friend or your partner

Join a group or a club (Yoga, Tai-Chi, bridge, gym, reading group, etc)

Give to charity

Volunteer your time

Be socially involved, be more trusting and loving, reach out

Exercise -Walk for 30 minutes a day, at least three times a week

Listen more carefully to your loved ones and others

Learn to be more attentive to things

(E.g. savor your food, enjoy your walk, feel the water on your body when having a shower, etc)

When you have set - backs try to look at the bright side

Learn to challenge your negative thoughts

Never lose hope – or be more hopeful

Category III

Undertake a project that you can get involved in – don't be too harsh on your time-lines

Embark on learning something new that you could enjoy and satisfy your curiosity. Gain competence in a new area, increasing your self-esteem and confidence

Join a worthwhile community project or volunteer your time for a worthwhile cause

Find more meaning in your life. If you are religiously inclined pray for others, attend your church, mosque or temple more. If you are not religious try to find awe and wonder in nature and appreciate the vastness of the cosmos or the beauty of every day events.

Practice mindfulness meditation as outlined in this book, or learn another form of meditation that appeals to you.

Practice loving kindness meditation or praying for others

Practice patient acceptance; try to be non-judgmental both for yourself and others

Further Reading and References

Authentic Happiness: Using the New Positive Psychology to Realize Your Potential for Lasting Fulfillment Author: Martin Seligman

Happiness: Unlocking the Mysteries of Psychological wealth Authors: Ed Diener, Robert Biswas-Diener

Positivity: Groundbreaking Research reveals How to Embrace the Hidden Strength of Positive Emotions Author: Barbara Fredrickson

The How of Happiness: A New Approach to Getting the Life You Want Author: Sonja Lyubomirsky

Flow: The Psychology of Optimal Experience Author: Mihaly Csikszentmihalyi

Happiness Hypothesis: Finding Modern Truth in Ancient Wisdom Author: Jonathan Haidt

What You Can Change and What You Can't: The Complete Guide to Successful Self-improvement   Author: Martin E. Seligman

Learned Optimism: How to Change Your Mind and Your Life: Author: Martin E. Seligman

The Art of Happiness: A Handbook of Living: Dalai Lama

Why Marriages Succeed or Fail: And How to Make Yours Last Author: John Gottman

Mindfulness-Based Cognitive Therapy for Depression: A New Approach to Preventing Relapse: Authors: Zindel V. Segel, Mark G. Williams, John D. Teasdale

Full Catastrophe Living: Using the Wisdom of Your Body and Mind to Face Stress, Pain and Illness   Author: Jon Kabat-Zinn

The Mindful Way Through Depression: Freeing Yourself from Chronic Unhappiness Authors: Mark Williams, John Teasdale, Zindel V. Segal, Jon Kabat-Zinn

The Compassionate Instinct: The Science of Human Goodness Authors: Authors: Dacher Keltner, Jason Marsh, Jeremy Adam Smith

Born to be Good: The Science of a Meaningful Life Author: Dacher Keltner

Compassionate Mind: Author: Paul Gilbert

Meaning, Medicine and the 'Placebo Effect' Author: Daniel E. Moerman

Buddha's Brain: The Practical Neuroscience of Happiness, Love and Wisdom Authors: Rick Hanson, Richard Mendrius

Peace is Every Step: The Path of Mindfulness in Everyday Life Author: Thich Nhat Hanh

Evidence Based Practice of Cognitive –Behavioral Therapy Authors: Deborah Dobson, Keith S. Dobson

Giving: How Each of us Can Change the World: Author: Bill Clinton

Bad Science: Ben Goldacre

SPEED MATHEMATICS USING THE VEDIC SYSTEM

By Vali Nasser

Can you multiply 994 X 996 mentally in 5 seconds?

Can you work out the square of 85 in 3 seconds without using a calculator?

Can you solve simultaneous equations in 45 seconds?

Speed Mathematics using the Vedic system makes learning basic mathematics more rewarding. The average pupil will be able to work out calculations such as 46X44, 95X95 and 116X114 mentally, often faster than a calculator. Pupils will understand how to work out squares, cubes, percentages, fractions, and equations with ease. Paper and pencil will still be required for most questions, but the speed and accuracy of calculations will improve significantly. This, in turn, will motivate pupils to learn more. This book provides smart strategies for mastering basic Number work and Algebra. These two areas are the building blocks in mathematics. Once pupils can master these aspects they will feel confident to tackle other branches of mathematics. This book is suitable for children from 10 to 16 years of age, but adults who want to improve the speed of mental calculations will also find this book useful.

You can order Speed Mathematics Using the Vedic System from any major bookshop or purchase online from Amazon or Barnes and Noble.

www.ingramcontent.com/pod-product-compliance
Ingram Content Group UK Ltd.
Pitfield, Milton Keynes, MK11 3LW, UK
UKHW041958230426
12048UKWH00008B/403